A DRINK OF ONE'S OWN

COCKTAILS FOR LITERARY LADIES

A DRINK OF ONE'S OWN

OF

ONE'S OWN

COCKTAILS FOR LITERARY LADIES

LAURA BECHERER AND
CAMEO MARLATT

ILLUSTRATED BY
SAVANNAH MARLATT

FREIGHT BOOKS

First published in the UK 2016
Freight Books
49 Virginia Street
Glasgow
G1 1TS

A CIP catalogue reference for this book is available from the
British Library.

ISBN 978-1-911332-08-4

Typeset by Freight Design Ltd
Printed and bound in Poland by Hussar Books.

the publisher acknowledges investment from
Creative Scotland toward the publication of this book

This book is dedicated to our mothers,
Connie Rae Zentner-Cline and Margaret Marlatt.

Thank you for teaching us how to be strong women.

We love you.

Contents

WEIGHTS AND MEASURES

Metric	Imperial	US cups
250ml	8 fl oz	1 cup
180ml	6 fl oz	¾ cup
150ml	5 fl oz	⅔ cup
120ml	4 fl oz	½ cup
75ml	2 ½ fl oz	⅓ cup
60ml	2 fl oz	¼ cup
30ml	1 fl oz	⅛ cup
15ml	½ fl oz	1 tablespoon

INTRODUCTION

A Drink of One's Own was created in a storm of feminist fury, born out of our frustration at the way the world has treated Zelda Fitzgerald and other creative women.

We were sitting at a table in our favorite Glaswegian pub one rainy night after class, drinking Laphroaig and discussing Kate Zambreno's *Heroines*. Zambreno's text explores Zelda Fitzgerald, among other women, and the way she was stifled and abused by her husband.

Fitzgerald endured a lot of bullying from Scott: he squashed her creativity, pushed her into an asylum, punished her for wanting to be an artist, plagiarized from her notebooks without her knowledge or permission, and threw a tantrum when she wrote a book about her own life and marriage before he could beat her to the punch. Ernest Hemingway also got involved in the debate; he once wrote an entire essay about measuring Scott's penis in a public restroom and comforting his wounded masculinity, stating that Zelda was trying to "destroy" Scott and his confidence.

What frustrates us the most is that history remembers Zelda as the overemotional and unstable half of the partnership and gives her little credit as a person in her own right. Even now, scholars talk about "Fitzgerald and Zelda," citing Zelda's work as of mild supplemental interest to those interested in Scott. Our own copy of Zelda Fitzgerald's novel, *Save Me the Waltz*, comes with a 50-year-old preface written by a fusty academic named Harry T. Moore, who spends the entire introduction to "Mrs. Fitzgerald's" book talking about her husband.

As we reflected on these injustices in the pub that evening, we began listing other women who have suffered similar fates. The Shelleys are another exasperating example. Many academics *still* insist that Percy Shelley must have written most of *Frankenstein*, or at least deserves equal credit in its creation, because Mary Shelley was "just a girl." Additionally, Mary Shelley is widely regarded as the first science fiction writer; she invented the genre with her creation of *Frankenstein*, yet women the world over struggle with being "allowed" into the realm of science fiction by white male gatekeepers. To add insult to injury, many adaptations of *Frankenstein* have twisted Shelley's original harrowing and heartbreaking tale of the neglected Other. Instead of the Creature being the center of the novel, used to explore humanity and the outcasts of humanity, the focus of the story becomes on Victor Frankenstein and his white male genius.

We thought of more and more women writers who have suffered this same fate. Dorothy Wordsworth. Hope Mirrlees. So many women of colour. And so, through our discussion, this cocktail book was formed. Partly because we had just read about the drinking culture of the Fitzgeralds, and partly because we were in a pub ourselves, we linked our anger over the way women are excluded from the literary world with the ways in which we are excluded from or policed in other coded-masculine realms as well, such as drinking culture and pubs. If we had a dime for every time 1) a male bartender has asked us, "Uh, you know that's a dark beer, right?", 2) a male patron has mansplained whisky to us, or 3) a strange bloke at the bar has interrupted our conversations with our male partners to explain the drinks menu to him over our own recommendations, we could afford to buy ourselves nicer gin. Drinking culture is especially linked with male writers like Ernest Hemingway and Scott Fitzgerald – women have been historically pushed away from the realm as a whole.

We wanted to devise a project that would give women a space of their own – or, more accurately, a book of their own. And we wanted the project to be fun, to be interesting and unique and uplifting, and to appeal to readers everywhere. We have created a space within these pages where the women included here can break free of the shadow of their male contemporaries and instead be celebrated as themselves.

This book is designed not only to give you great cocktail recipes, but to offer you a selection of amazing, talented, diverse women writers. Some of them are very popular and you'll recognize them immediately. Others are less well known. All are worth reading, and we've provided several recommendations for you in these pages as well. We want you to not only discover new drinks, but new books and writers as well.

With that goal in mind, we focused on international representation when selecting our authors. We were particularly dedicated to including women of colour, because while all women suffer from sexism in publishing, women of colour get slammed with double invisibility and erasure due to racism. Publicized feminism is still overwhelmingly the realm of white (and cishet, wealthy, able-bodied) women. We tried to strike a better balance of identities here, and although the end result is far from perfect, we do hope you enjoy the variety.

While some of our cocktails require expensive or unusual ingredients, many of them were made with the specific intention of keeping the drinks affordable and easy to make. A problem we've noticed with many cocktail and cookbooks is that their recipes often rely on expensive or hard-to-find ingredients. Although we hope that our book will be enjoyed by drinks connoisseurs, we also focused our attention on creating recipes that would be easily accessible to regular, run-of-the-mill folks who enjoy good books and tasty drinks.

Happy reading, and happy mixing!
Laura and Cameo

A GUIDE TO LIQUOR INFUSIONS

While you can buy many types of flavoured vodkas, they are often overpriced and the selection and quality limited. Infusing your own is more fun, more creative and more cost-effective.

One can infuse almost anything into vodka or white rum. The quality will depend upon the quality of the liquor you use, but even a cheap vodka or rum can be infused to make a potent and tasty cocktail base. If you want to experiment, don't be afraid to get a store brand bottle of vodka and try out several combinations.

Fruits make great liquor infusions – in this book, we use several fruit infusions like apple and plum to give you excellent recipes. Herbs are also a good source – we have created infusions using mint, lavender, and thyme. We encourage you to use your imagination and try out whatever takes your fancy – ginger, pear, melon, basil, cucumber. The possibilities are almost endless, and many of our cocktails can easily swap out one infusion for another if you would prefer a different flavor.

To infuse a liquor, put a handful of fruit or herbs in the bottom of a clean glass jar. Pour the jar full of your desired liquor, cover it with a tight-fitting lid, and give it a good shake. Leave it to infuse for 3–5 days in a dark, cool space, giving it a good shake about once a day. Once your infusion has reached your desired level of potency, strain out the solids and enjoy!

A GUIDE TO
SIMPLE SYRUPS

Simple syrups are easy to make and nearly as versatile as liquor infusions. Pour equal parts sugar and water (often one cup and one cup) into a saucepan and stir. Bring to the boil, then simmer on a low heat for about 10 minutes until the mixture thickens. To create a flavoured syrup, try adding fruits or herbs to sugar. Some of our recipes suggest basil or lavender, but here again is a place for you to experiment. After the syrup has thickened, strain out the solids and start mixing!

Some of our recipes also call for honey syrup – this is even easier to make than simple syrup. While you can make the syrup by adding equal parts honey and water to a pan and following the instructions above, we've found it works almost as well to add honey to an equal part of boiling water and briskly stir until the honey is dissolved.

The Harper Lee cocktail, page 22

NORTH AMERICA

ZELDA FITZGERALD
1900 – 1948

Zelda Sayre Fitzgerald, the original flapper, was our inspiration for this book.

She was married to American author F. Scott Fitzgerald, and the combination of 20th century society and Scott's massive ego left Zelda stifled by her husband and his obsession with success. In addition to basing many of his female characters on Zelda, and using their conversations for dialogue in his novels, Fitzgerald also plagiarized Zelda, lifting entire passages from her journals to furnish his creative work. When Zelda tried to become creative in her own right, through ballet and writing, Scott grew wildly jealous. She was committed to an asylum, and 'diagnosed' with schizophrenia. Labelling women, crazy, is an age-old way to silence women who are misbehaving in the eyes of their male partners. While committed, Zelda wrote her own novel, *Save Me the Waltz*. The novel was based loosely on her own life, which enraged Scott, as he was using Zelda's story for his own novel, *Tender is the Night*. Today, people largely remember Zelda in relation to her husband, and some scholarly rhetoric still casts a victim-blaming light on her drinking and mental health misdiagnoses. It is our hope that this book will serve as a tribute to Zelda and stand as a testimony that women deserve to be recognized as individuals in their own right.

In Zelda's honour, we present you with this gin-based twist on a Prohibition classic. Before you drink it, raise your glass to Zelda; toast her and all other women whose identities have been consumed by their husbands.

THE
ZELDA FITZGERALD COCKTAIL

Recipe
- 1 ½ fl oz gin
- 1 fl oz honey syrup
- 1 fl oz ginger beer
- ½ fl oz lemon juice

To make the honey syrup, stir honey into an equal part of hot water until dissolved.

Refrigerate the leftovers. Combine all ingredients and stir well. Pour into a highball glass over ice.

Notable works:
Save Me the Waltz, Scandalabra, Bits of Paradise

TONI MORRISON

1931 – Present

Toni Morrison is a Black American author from Ohio who, like many of our other authors, needs little explanation on her literary brilliance. Morrison is Professor Emeritus at Princeton University, an editor, and a novelist. *The Bluest Eye* and *Beloved* are our top recommendations – both books that delve deep into their characters' psyches. Morrison, like many women of colour authors, writes eloquently on the bitterly painful topics of race, gender, and oppression. Her characters are rich and her narratives as rewarding as they are important testimonies to the experiences of Black Americans. Morrison was awarded the Nobel Prize in Literature in 1993.

Morrison's cocktail gives you an opportunity to practise your flavoured simple syrups. A standard vodka tonic is given new life with basil syrup and fresh cucumber. Perfect for a sunshine-filled afternoon on the back deck with a stack of Morrison's novels next to your elbow.

THE
TONI MORRISON COCKTAIL

Recipe
- 1 ½ fl oz vodka
- 3 fl oz tonic water
- 1 spoonful basil syrup
- several fresh basil leaves to garnish
- cucumber slices to garnish

To make syrup, add ½ cup water and ½ cup sugar to small saucepan. Add 6 – 8 fresh basil leaves. Bring to boil, then simmer for 10 minutes. Strain out basil. Pour vodka over ice, add syrup. Add tonic water, stir. Garnish with basil leaves and cucumber slices.

Notable works:
The Bluest Eye, Beloved, Sula, Song of Solomon, Tar Baby, A Mercy, Jazz, Home, Playing in the Dark

EMILY DICKINSON

1830 – 1886

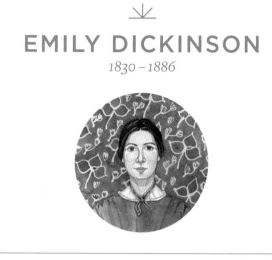

Though she is now thought of as one of the most distinct and formative voices in American literature, 19th century poet Emily Dickinson was almost entirely unrecognized during her lifetime, having published less than a dozen poems. Those works, and the collections published after her death, were heavily edited to conform to the stylistic conventions of the time. Today her poetry is known for its treatment of nature, its preoccupation with mortality and its unusual punctuation, most notably a generous use of the dash. Dickinson was also a prolific letter writer, owing largely to her reclusive and introverted nature. It is said that she rarely left her house, or even her room, in the final years of her life. However, she was also a dedicated gardener and amateur botanist, the influence of which is strong in her work, and this recipe, which would not be complete without a few 'dashes' of lavender bitters.

When asked by a friend for a description of herself, she said she was 'small, like the Wren; and my Hair is bold, like the Chestnut Bur – and my eyes, like the Sherry in the Glass, that the Guest leaves.' Thinking of this, we have chosen a base of nutty Amontillado sherry combined with elderflower liqueur to create a drink that is deep amber in tone and floral in flavor. Garnish it, if you can, with a sprig of lavender or other edible flower, such as a violet. Simple yet complex, this drink is the perfect tribute to one of literature's greatest poets.

THE
EMILY DICKINSON COCKTAIL

Recipe
- 2 fl oz amontillado sherry
- ¾ fl oz elderflower liqueur
- 2 dashes lavender bitters
- edible flower to garnish

In a cocktail shaker, combine the sherry, liqueur, and bitters with ice and shake thoroughly. Strain into a chilled sherry glass. Garnish with an edible flower, such as a violet or sprig of lavender.

Notable works:
Hope Is The Thing With Feathers, A Book, "Why Do I Love" You, Sir?, A Bird Came Down

MAYA ANGELOU

1928 – 2014

With a writer as prolific, acclaimed, and beloved as Maya Angelou, it's hard to know where to begin. Her awards are too numerous to list, and she has received over fifty honorary degrees. You probably know her best for the book that made her famous: *I Know Why the Caged Bird Sings*. Published in 1969, this autobiography deals with the racism and traumatic rape she experienced as a child. It was the first of seven that she would complete during her lifetime, writing in an episodic and unique literary style that has changed the face of American memoir. Though she is better known for her prose, Angelou considered herself a poet and playwright before she started writing her autobiographies, and was nominated for a Pulitzer Prize for her 1971 collection *Just Give me a Cool Drink of Water 'fore I Diiie*. She also read her poem 'On the Pulse of Morning' at Bill Clinton's presidential inauguration in 1993, resulting in a huge increase in her popularity. And no biography of Angelou would be complete without mention of her civil rights activism, which saw her working with Malcolm X and Martin Luther King, Jr. It was in the wake of their assassinations that she wrote *I Know Why the Caged Bird Sings*.

Angelou's writing process famously involved locking herself in a hotel room with a bottle of sherry, so we've added a dash to this delicious cocktail, which is a sweet and uplifting blend of white rum and pineapple juice.

THE
MAYA ANGELOU COCKTAIL

Recipe
- 1 ½ fl oz white rum
- 2 fl oz pineapple juice
- 1 tsp grenadine
- 1 tsp amontillado sherry
- maraschino cherry to garnish

In a cocktail shaker, combine rum, juice, grenadine and sherry. Shake with ice and strain into a chilled lowball glass. Garnish with a maraschino cherry.

Notable works:
I Know Why the Caged Bird Sings, Just Give me a Cool Drink of Water 'fore I Diiie, And Still I Rise

MARGARET ATWOOD
1939 – Present

We had the occasion to meet Margaret Atwood and ask her which cocktail she would like to be for this book. In true Atwood fashion, she gave us her cryptic, somewhat intimidating smile and told us we could decide for ourselves.

Margaret Atwood is a personal heroine. *Lady Oracle*, our top recommendation, was published in 1976 yet still has the power to speak directly to us in terms of our lives as women. Atwood writes across a variety of genres, from the speculative fiction of *The Handmaid's Tale* to the historical exploration of *Alias Grace* to the layered narratives of *The Blind Assassin*. Atwood is one of the most versatile writers in the English language: she rewrote mythology to give Penelope a voice, put realist twists on fairy tales, is a poet, and has published volumes of essays. She has proven her ability to adapt her writing to keep on top of ever-changing social and political issues, and she never shies away from unapologetic feminism.

Given permission to create our own Atwood cocktail, we opted for hot buttered rum with Canadian maple syrup. Perfect for those cozy winter nights when you settle in for a long evening with her latest book.

THE
MARGARET ATWOOD
COCKTAIL

Recipe
- 8 tbsp butter
- ¾ cup brown sugar
- ¾ cup pure maple syrup
- 1 tsp nutmeg
- 1 tsp vanilla extract
- 1 bottle (750 ml) brandy
- 3 cups boiling water
- 4 whole cinnamon sticks

Melt butter in saucepan over medium heat. Add sugar and nutmeg, stir until sugar has melted. Remove from heat. Add brandy and vanilla to saucepan, stir continuously. Add boiling water and cinnamon sticks, stir. Return to burner. Add maple syrup, stir over low heat to mix. Leave pot on very low heat to keep warm, serve in warm mugs.

Note: Make sure you use pure maple syrup for this recipe; the imitation brands will not turn out well.

Notable works:
Lady Oracle, The Handmaid's Tale, The Blind Assassin, Alias Grace, Surfacing, The Robber Bride, The Penelopiad, the Maddaddam trilogy, The Heart Goes Last, Bluebeard's Egg, Stone Mattress, Murder in the Dark, The Door

URSULA LE GUIN

1929 – Present

What can we even say about Ursula Le Guin in these pages that will do her justice? Le Guin is known for both her fantasy and science fiction, and she particularly stands out as a feminist author who is willing to grow. Le Guin never rewrites her narratives; she simply changes her ideology with each new book she writes. Le Guin now lives in the States with her husband, she still keeps an active blog in which she offers criticism on the literary world as well as the detailed adventures of her time-travelling cat, Pard.

Whether your imagination prefers to dwell in Earthsea or Anarres, our Ursula Le Guin cocktail will take you to an otherworldy place.

THE
<u>URSULA LE GUIN</u>
COCKTAIL

Recipe
- 2 fl oz rum
- ½ fl oz triple-sec
- 2 tsp lavender syrup
- 2 dashes bitters

In a cocktail shaker, combine ingredients with ice and shake. Strain into an old-fashioned glass.

Notable works:
The Earthsea Quartet, Lavinia, Annals of the Western Shore, The Dispossessed

AMY TAN

1952 – Present

Amy Tan is a deeply comforting writer. She is best known for her first novel, *The Joy Luck Club,* but *The Hundred Secret Senses* and *The Kitchen God's Wife* are our particular favourites. Tan writes beautifully about women and mother/ daughter relationships, as well as about the struggles of being Chinese-American. Themes of family, identity, and the struggle that comes with falling between two cultures and languages are present in all of her works, and her words strike a vivid and magical pose on the page.

When we think of Amy Tan we can't help but think of oranges, which are a good luck food in many of her novels. Tan's writing is deep and sharp, yet light and filled with clarity. Her books weigh comfortably in our hands with the same balance and satisfaction of an orange.

For Tan, then, we have created a fragrant orange-flavoured version of the vodka tonic. Orange-infused vodka, Cointreau, and a touch of orange blossom water balance out the bitterness of the tonic water to give you a refreshing, sun-filled drink.

THE
AMY TAN
COCKTAIL

Recipe
- 2 fl oz orange-infused vodka
- 2 tbsp Cointreau
- 1 tbsp orange flower water
- 3 fl oz tonic water
- orange slices (with peel) to garnish

Combine vodka, Cointreau, orange flower water, and tonic water. Pour over ice and garnish with orange slices.

Notable works:
The Joy Luck Club, The Hundred Secret Senses, The Kitchen God's Wife, The Valley of Amazement

LOUISE ERDRICH

1954 – Present

Louise Erdrich is an Ojibwe novelist and poet from Little Falls, Minnesota. Her novels focus on the lives of Native American characters, often concentrating on themes of family and tribal history. Erdrich's novels contain strong elements of magical realism, resulting in narratives that dance across the borders between magic, religion, nature, and humanity.

We love Erdrich because she is an unapologetic advocate for her community. Her writing is beautiful, stunning, and unforgettable in its honesty and empathy; we cannot recommend her novels highly enough.

Because Erdrich often writes about the problems of alcoholism, we have elected to give her a non-alcoholic cocktail. Blackberries feature in this drink, because blackberry picking is a summer ritual in much of the Midwest. This blackberry iced tea recipe is the perfect companion for you when you crack open *Love Medicine*.

THE
LOUISE ERDRICH COCKTAIL

Recipe
- 6 cups cold water
- 4 breakfast tea bags
- 3 cups fresh blackberries
- 1 cup sugar
- 1 tbsp fresh, chopped mint
- mint leaf to garnish

In a large pitcher, soak 4 teabags in cold water overnight in the refrigerator. (Alternatively, let steep in the warm sun all day, remove tea bags, and chill overnight). Next day, combine blackberries, sugar, and mint in a container, let sit for half an hour. Stir well into pitcher of tea, let stand at room temperature for one hour. Strain. Serve in tall glasses over ice with mint leaf garnish. Spoon strained fruit over warm custard or vanilla ice cream.

Notable works:
The Round House, LaRose, Love Medicine, Tracks, The Plague of Doves, The Painted Drum

DOROTHY PARKER

1893 – 1967

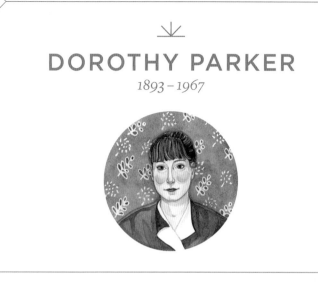

Dorothy Parker is undoubtedly the wittiest author on our list. Her literary career began in 1914 when her first poem was published in Vanity Fair, for whom she later worked at as a staff writer. There, she met several of the authors with whom she would found the famous Algonquin Round Table, a group of collaborators who met regularly at New York's Algonquin Hotel. Soon enough, she and her wit had developed a national reputation, and she became famous for her sharp-tongued comedic poems on the topics of romance, death and, of course, drinking. Though she is most well known for her verse, she was also a skilled short story writer and an accomplished screenwriter, receiving an Academy Award nomination for contributing to the screenplay of the 1937 film *A Star is Born*. However, she was ultimately placed on the Hollywood blacklist due to her socialist politics. Parker is as popular today as she has ever been. *The Portable Dorothy Parker* stands alongside the Bible and Shakespeare as the only of Viking Press's 'Portable Library' series to remain continuously in print.

Nothing but a classic Manhattan cocktail would suit this true New Yorker, but we've added a black pepper twist as a wink to her wise-cracking humour.

THE
DOROTHY PARKER
COCKTAIL

Recipe
- 2 fl oz rye
- ¾ fl oz sweet vermouth
- 1–3 dashes bitters
- ½ tsp black pepper syrup
- 1 maraschino cherry to garnish

For the black pepper syrup, heat sugar and water until the sugar has dissolved. Add whole peppercorns and continue to heat until the mixture tastes strongly of pepper.

Combine rye, vermouth, syrup, and bitters in a cocktail shaker. Shake with ice until very cold, and strain into a chilled martini glass. Garnish with a maraschino cherry.

Notable works:
The Collected Dorothy Parker, Dorothy Parker – Complete Stories

The Alice Munro cocktail, page 38

The Chimamanda Ngozi Adichie cocktail, page 116

HARPER LEE

1926 – 2016

Harper Lee is one of the greatest American authors of all time, and one of the most well-known. Although *Go Set a Watchman* was recently released, we still think of Lee as primarily a one-novel genius – a perception justified by the fact that both novels were originally one. *To Kill a Mockingbird* tells such a powerful story that we felt it important to include her here. Lee's narrative, told from the point of view of a child, is unforgettable in American social and literary consciousness. Lee was also a recluse, a writer who refused fame and wanted only to be left to live her life.

Lee's cocktail reminds one of the American South, drawing on peaches and bourbon to create a full-flavoured drink. Bitters prevents it from becoming overly sweet, and champagne brings all the notes into a perfect balance.

THE
HARPER LEE
COCKTAIL

Recipe
- 1 ½ fl oz bourbon
- 1 ½ fl oz peach liqueur
- bitters
- champagne
- peach slice to garnish

Combine bourbon and peach liqueur. Add bitters, stir. Pour over ice into champagne flute, top off with champagne, and garnish with peach slice.

Notable works:
To Kill a Mockingbird, Go Set a Watchman

SYLVIA PLATH

1932 – 1963

Born in Boston, Massachusetts, in 1932, Sylvia Plath was from a young age driven in her education and literary ambitions, publishing her first poems as child and achieving academic success as a student at Smith College, despite battling severe clinical depression. Her semi-autobiographical novel *The Bell Jar* reflects these experiences, depicting an ambitious young woman's struggle with mental illness and patriarchal oppression in 1950s America.

While attending Cambridge University in 1956, Plath met and married fellow poet Ted Hughes. Their tumultuous relationship is the source of much debate over Hughes' influence on Plath's writing and mental health. Plath's most famous poetry collection, *Ariel*, was written in the period following her separation from Hughes, and published posthumously after her suicide in 1963. Plath's literary accomplishments are legion, and include helping to establish the confessional genre of poetry, and winning a posthumous Pulitzer Prize in 1982. She stands as one of the 20th century's most popular poets.

For our Sylvia Plath cocktail, we've put a raspberry twist on a lesser-known American classic: the Pink Lady. Much like Plath's oeuvre, this strong and complex drink has suffered historical critique by male cocktail critics for its feminine name and appearance. With just enough grenadine and cream to create its signature pink colour, this is a biting gin martini in a 1950s frock which, for us, reflects the conflict between playful form and violent content present in Plath's poetry.

THE
SYLVIA PLATH
COCKTAIL

Recipe
- 1 ½ fl oz gin
- 1 tsp grenadine
- 1 tbsp cream
- 1 egg white
- 1 tsp raspberry coulis
- raspberry to garnish

For the raspberry coulis, larger quantities can be made by blending a package of raspberries with 2 tablespoons of sugar in a food processor. For individual cocktails, use a fork to blend a few raspberries with a teaspoon of sugar in a small bowl. In both cases, strain the mixture through a sieve to remove seeds.

Combine gin, grenadine, cream, and egg white in a cocktail shaker. Shake with ice until chilled. Pour raspberry coulis into the bottom of a chilled martini glass, and strain the cocktail mixture over the top. Garnish with a fresh raspberry.

Notable works:
The Bell Jar, Ariel, The Colossus and Other Poems, Crossing the Water, Letters Home

CHARLOTTE PERKINS GILMAN

1860 – 1935

Charlotte Perkins Gilman is the author of one of our most beloved novellas, 'The Yellow Wallpaper'. Gilman was an American writer and feminist born in 1860. 'The Yellow Wallpaper' is a scathing critique of the way doctors and the medical system in general treated female patients – gaslighting, control, and diagnoses of "hysteria" ran rampant. Gilman also wrote *Herland*, the feminist utopian novel that offers its readers a picture of what an ideal, gender-balanced society may look like.

We love Gilman for her feminism. It's open, it's blunt, and it's undeniable on the page. 'The Yellow Wallpaper' is a story that many recognize by name only; we encourage you to drop what you're doing and read it now. We also encourage you to have a Charlotte Perkins Gilman cocktail while you read. Gilman's cocktail is as classic as her writing – a slight twist on the pink gin, a popular ladies' drink in mid-19th century England. Don't expect sweetness or frivolity – the Charlotte Perkins Gilman cocktail is a pairing of gin and bitters that will turn your drink rose-coloured. Add a sprig of rosemary for a fragrant and sharp garnish.

THE
CHARLOTTE PERKINS GILMAN COCKTAIL

Recipe
- 3 fl oz gin
- dash Angostura bitters
- rosemary sprig to garnish

Shake gin and bitters with ice, strain into martini glass. Add rosemary sprig to garnish.

Notable works:
The Yellow Wallpaper, Herland, The Crux, Women and Economics, In This Our World

JAMAICA KINCAID
1949 – Present

Jamaica Kincaid is an Antiguan-American author and gardener who writes novels and essays as well as gardening texts. She was born in St. John's, Antigua into poverty. She was educated in Antigua and later made her way to the United States, where she eventually obtained a position writing for *The New Yorker*. Her famous prose-poem, 'Girl', was published by *The New Yorker* in 1978. Notable novels we recommend are *Lucy* and *The Autobiography of my Mother*.

Kincaid's writing style is incredibly rich and evocative, made more poignant through its simplicity. Kincaid is one of our favourite authors because criticism against her often comes in the form of the complaint that 'she's too angry'. If anyone has a right to be angry, we feel it's probably a Black woman who grew up in a colonialist country and from there moved to the United States. Kincaid is angry – and she should be. We love her anger, and we encourage you to give her a read and love her anger as well.

Antigua is known for its pineapples, and therefore we have created a pineapple cocktail for Kincaid. It is tart, sweet, and potent all at the same time – much like her writing. The sweetness of the pineapple is balanced well with the rum and lime. Have one while reading 'Girl' aloud to your friends; it's an experience you won't regret.

THE
JAMAICA KINCAID
COCKTAIL

Recipe
- Jamaica Kincaid
- 1 ½ fl oz dark rum
- 2 fl oz pineapple juice
- 1 fl oz coconut milk
- lime wedge

Combine rum, pineapple juice, and coconut milk.
Pour into glass over ice and squeeze in lime wedge.

Notable works:
*Lucy, The Autobiography of my Mother, Annie John,
A Small place, See Now Then*

GWENDOLYN BROOKS

1917 – 2000

Born in 1917, this brilliant American writer is known for her politically engaged and formally diverse poetry. When Brooks was a child, her family moved to Chicago, the city that would provide endless inspiration over the course of her writing life. Encouraged by supportive parents, Brooks was determined to become a poet at a young age, and began publishing while still in her teens. In 1945 she published her first collection of poetry, *A Street in Bronzeville*; with technical mastery and intense energy, she wrote about what she saw on the streets of Chicago's South Side, examining what it meant to be poor and black in 1940s America. The book was highly praised, and she was lauded as an important new voice in American poetry. In 1946, she was awarded her first Guggenheim Fellowship, and in 1950 she became the first African American author to win a Pulitzer Prize for her collection *Annie Allen*. This book, which shows Brooks joyfully experimenting with form, follows a girl dealing with racism and gender oppression as she grows into womanhood. Brooks' work, already socially engaged, grew even more so alongside the civil rights movement in the 1960s. This consciousness is perhaps best realized in her powerful work *In the Mecca*, which was nominated for the National Book Award for Poetry in 1968.

A poet this good needs a drink with real kick, and we can guarantee that this 'mocktail' mix of spicy ginger beer, tart lime juice, and minty sweet syrup is as lively as Brooks' verse.

THE
GWENDOLYN BROOKS COCKTAIL

Recipe
- 5 fl oz ginger beer
- ½ fl oz lime juice
- ½ fl oz mint syrup
- cucumber slices
- fresh mint to garnish

Combine lime juice and syrup. Pour over ice and cucumber slices in a chilled Collins glass. Add ginger beer. Top with a sprig of mint for garnish.

Notable works:
Annie Allen, Maud Martha, A Street in Bronzeville, Aloneness, The Bean Eaters, To Disembark

SANDRA CISNEROS

1954 – Present

Sandra Cisneros is an American writer with a Mexican-American family background. She was born in Chicago, Illinois in 1954 and is a key contributor to Chicana literature. Cisneros writes about identity, gender and class; her work explores the feeling of living in the space in-between two cultures. Cisneros is best known for her novel *The House on Mango Street.*

We love women who write about their identities. Chicana literature is vital for millions of American readers who struggle with racism and displaced cultural identity. One could argue that America as a nation is not kind toward its people of colour. Cisneros and other Chicana writers are essential; they explore the lives of marginalized Americans with an honesty that is stamped out and silenced in the larger North American literary conversation.

The Sandra Cisneros cocktail is an alcoholic version of traditional Mexican Agua Fresca. In this case we have chosen to use watermelon as our fruit base and have added tequila. This is a versatile drink that can be enjoyed with or without alcohol and can be altered depending on what fruit you like best.

THE
SANDRA CISNEROS COCKTAIL

Recipe
- 4 cups cubed seedless watermelon
- 2 tbsp white sugar
- 10–12 fresh mint leaves
- 8 cups cold water
- 1 lime, wedged
- 1 fl oz tequila (per glass) (optional)
- champagne (optional)

Mix together watermelon, sugar, mint leaves, and one cup of water. Cover bowl with plastic wrap and refrigerate for about 4 hours. Remove and mash mixture well with a fork. Add remaining water, mix well. To make alcoholic, add 1 fl oz tequila and/or a splash of champagne to each glass. However, this drink can easily be enjoyed alcohol-free. Garnish each glass with a lime wedge.

This recipe also works with other fruits, so feel free to experiment.

Notable works:
The House on Mango Street, Woman Hollering Creek, Caramelo, Have You Seen Marie?

JULIA ALVAREZ

1950 – Present

Julia Alvarez is a Dominican-American poet and novelist, considered to be one of the world's most significant Latina writers. Though born in New York City, Alvarez spent the first ten years of her life in the Dominican Republic, where her family is from. When her father became involved in a failed attempt to overthrow the dictator Rafael Trujillo, they were forced to flee the country and return to the United States. These political circumstances, and the difficult cultural transition, would influence her most acclaimed novels, *How the Garcia Girls Lost Their Accents* and *In the Time of the Butterflies*. Alvarez began her literary career writing poetry, publishing her collection *The Homecoming* in 1984, a book that looks back to her childhood and celebrates the details of domestic life. Her work is known for examining the cultural expectations of Dominican American women, and violence against women.

One episode in *How the Garcia Girls Lost Their Accents* involves a character, Yolanda, returning to the Dominican Republic from America. In an effort to recapture her roots, she decides to go guava picking, so it is only appropriate that this cocktail have guava juice for its base. Combined with gin and basil syrup, this drink evokes the setting so central to Alvarez's work.

THE
JULIA ALVAREZ
COCKTAIL

Recipe
- 1 ½ fl oz gin
- 3 fl oz guava juice
- 1 tsp basil syrup
- basil sprig to garnish

For the basil syrup, combine water and sugar and heat on the stovetop. Stir until the sugar has dissolved, add a handful of basil leaves, and keep on low heat until the syrup tastes strongly of basil.

Combine gin, guava juice, and basil syrup over ice in a cocktail shaker. Shake and strain into a lowball glass. Run a basil leaf around the rim, and garnish with a fresh sprig.

Notable works:
How the Garcia Girls Lost Their Accents, *In the Time of the Butterflies*, *The Homecoming*

ALICE WALKER

1944 – Present

Alice Walker is, in a word, remarkable. She is a novelist, a short story writer, a poet, and an activist. Our favourite of her books, *The Color Purple*, won her the National Book Award and the Pulitzer Prize for fiction in 1983. Walker is a Black writer from Georgia, USA, who overcame great poverty and institutional racism to become one of the world's most famous and important writers on the subjects of humanity and injustice.

The Color Purple is one of the most astonishing novels we have ever read. It is so sad and uplifting at the same time – one cannot help but cry throughout. Exploring from deep trauma to profound bonds of love, the narrative weaves such a beautiful web that the pain depicted is inseparable from the joy. *The Color Purple* is an epistolary novel written almost like an oral tale – a tradition that Walker learned in her childhood – in that its speaker, Celie, writes in her natural speech patterns. The result brings Celie and her supporting characters to life in a way that few writers can accomplish – the words virtually sing off the page. Race, gender, and female sexuality are openly explored in this text; Celie and Sugar's relationship is possibly the most heart-capturing love story we know.

With *The Color Purple* in mind, we created a cocktail that to us encapsulates the relationship between Celie and Sugar. Fresh rhubarb and strawberry remind us of Celie's rural upbringing, and the champagne represents Sugar's glamour.

THE
ALICE WALKER
COCKTAIL

Recipe
- 1 cup plain or
  flavoured yogurt
- 1 cup diced rhubarb
- 1 cup strawberries
- 2 tsp fresh mint
- chilled champagne
- mint to garnish

Add yogurt, rhubarb, strawberries, and mint
to a blender and blend. Pour into tall glasses or
Mason jars, top with champagne, and slowly stir to
combine. Garnish with mint.

Almost any fruit combination may be used for this
recipe, so don't be afraid to experiment! Other ideas
include using combinations of raspberry, banana,
blueberry, blackberry, mango, pineapple, peach, etc.

Notable works:
*The Third Life of Grange Copeland, The Color Purple,
Meridian, The Temple of My Familiar*

ALICE MUNRO
1931 – Present

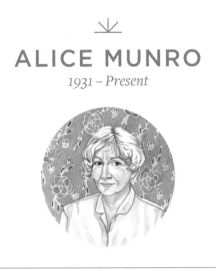

When it comes to short stories, few writers can top the subtlety and psychological nuance of Alice Munro, who in 2013 became the first Canadian to win a Nobel Prize for Literature. But Munro is no stranger to literary awards: her first collection, *Dance of the Happy Shades,* won a Governor General's Award, as did two of her subsequent books. This well-deserved critical acclaim is partly a result of Munro's attention to social detail in portraying the culture of her native Huron County, Ontario, where much of her fiction is set. From the girls coming of age in her early work, to the older women of her recent publications, Munro's complex female characters strive beyond the religious and cultural traditions of their small-town homes. It is safe to say that this brilliant author has revolutionized the short story form.

The Alice Munro cocktail is our take on a Blueberry Tea cocktail, a liqueur-based drink served with hot tea in a brandy snifter. Rather than the traditional black breakfast tea, we substitute Earl Grey to compliment the Cointreau. This fruity and comforting cocktail is perfect for those cold Canadian winters, with a few fresh blueberries tossed in to remind you of summer.

THE
ALICE MUNRO COCKTAIL

Recipe
– 1 fl oz amaretto liqueur
– 1 fl oz Cointreau
– 4 fl oz hot Earl Grey tea
– blueberries to garnish

In a brandy snifter, combine the liqueurs and hot tea. Add a few blueberries for garnish.

Notable works:
Dance of the Happy Shades, Dear Life, Runway, To Much Happiness, The View from Castle Rock

PAULINE JOHNSON

1861 – 1913

Pauline Johnson, also known by her Mohawk name, Tekahionwake, is an important figure in Canadian cultural history. Born in 1861 to a Mohawk chief father and an English immigrant mother, Johnson had a mixed race ancestry that would deeply inform her work as a writer and performer. Her father's leading social position meant that her upbringing was privileged, and as a sickly child she was educated at home, avoiding the trauma of attending one of Canada's problematic residential schools for Native children. Despite the deep-seated racism of the time, her parents encouraged her to learn about both sides of her heritage and she grew up listening to the Mohawk language stories of her paternal grandfather, John Smoke Johnson, who had a great influence on her career. Beginning in the 1880s, she published poems prolifically in national periodicals and began performing them on stage. Though very popular in her time, her work fell out of favour until the late-20th century when feminist and postcolonial critics took an interest in her themes of race and gender. Now she is recognized for her significant contribution to Canadian literature.

Our Pauline Johnson cocktail is a cool, sweet blend of pear juice and vodka, with crème de cacao taking center stage. Theatrical and elegant, just like its namesake.

THE
PAULINE JOHNSON
COCKTAIL

Recipe
- 1 ½ fl oz vodka
- ¼ fl oz crème de cacao
- 5 fl oz pear juice
- mint sprig to garnish

Combine vodka, crème de cacao, and pear juice.
Pour over ice in a Collins glass. Add a mint sprig
for garnish.

Notable works:
*Legends of Vancouver, Flint and Feather, Tekahionwake,
The White Wampum, The Moccasin Maker*

UNITED KINGDOM

ANGELA CARTER

1940 – 1992

Angela Carter was a second-wave feminist author most well-known for her sensual and explicit reinterpretations of fairy tales. Her novels, such as *Nights at the Circus*, and short story collections, such as *Saints and Strangers*, make use of magical realism and the surreal. Carter's distinct writing style has been described by Margaret Atwood as 'baroque', a label that connotes her rich language and vivid imagery. Whether she is rewriting classic tales like Beauty and the Beast, reinterpreting notorious figures like Lizzy Borden, or crafting tales around legends like the German Erlkönig, Carter gives her material fantastical, usually bloody, twists that often explore the female body.

To honour our favourite collection of Carter stories, *The Bloody Chamber*, we have selected a Bloody Mary recipe for the Angela Carter cocktail. Mix up this thick, spicy treat and kick back with a volume of macabre feminist reflections full of lady vampires, errant wolves and gratuitous amounts of blood.

THE
ANGELA CARTER
COCKTAIL

Recipe
- 6 fl oz tomato juice
- 1 ½ fl oz beetroot-
  infused vodka
- 2 dashes
  Worcestershire sauce
- 2 dashes hot pepper
  sauce
- 1 dash steak sauce
- 1 dash grated
  horseradish
- 1 clove roasted garlic
- pinch of celery salt
- pinch of sea salt
- squeeze of lime
- black pepper to taste

Mix all ingredients well and pour over ice in a highball or other tall glass.

Garnish with celery, pickles, olives, and/or pickled okra.

Notable works:
Nights at the Circus, Saints and Strangers, The Bloody Chamber, Wise Children

VIRGINIA WOOLF

1882 – 1941

The inspiration for the title of this book, Virginia Woolf's *A Room of One's Own* is a classic of early feminist literature that explores the financial, social and psychological limitations faced by women writers throughout history. Within the progressive environment of the Bloomsbury Group of London intellectuals, Woolf wrote such novels as *To the Lighthouse* and *Mrs Dalloway*, known today for their masterful lyricism, formal innovation, and treatment of women's lived experience. She also explored themes of lesbianism, most notably in *Orlando*, the long-lived gender-swapping title character of which was based on Woolf's lover Vita Sackville-West.

So raise a glass to the queen of British Modernism: light as Clarissa Dalloway's floral arrangements, strong as an existential crisis, this gin cocktail is Woolfian through and through.

THE
VIRGINIA WOOLF COCKTAIL

Recipe
- 2 fl oz gin
- 4 fl oz sparkling
  lemonade
- sliced cucumber
- lime slice

In a Collins glass, pour gin and lemonade over ice.
Muddle in a slice or two of cucumber and add a slice
of lime if desired.

Notable works:
Mrs Dalloway, *To the Lighthouse*, *Orlando*,
A Room of One's Own

JANE AUSTEN

1775 – 1817

She may have been writing in Regency England, but Jane Austen's social comedy and piercing insight into human nature has yet to go out of style. With characteristic nuance, depth and humour, Austen gives female relationships center stage in her novels, from *Pride and Prejudice* to *Sense and Sensibility*. Beneath her light-hearted marriage plots, we see Austen's heroines struggle to achieve the social and financial stability of marriage in a culture that denies them independence.

This gin-based cocktail is topped with pink champagne to reflect Austen's sparkling wit. It's light, it's feminine and it packs the punch of an underhanded drawing room insult delivered straight from Elizabeth Bennet's mouth.

THE
JANE AUSTEN COCKTAIL

Recipe
- 2 fl oz gin
- 2 dashes rose water
- 2 tsp earl grey tea syrup
- pink champagne or sparkling wine

In a cocktail shaker, mix the gin, rose water, and syrup. Shake with ice. Drain into a chilled martini glass and top with pink champagne.

Notable works:
Pride and Prejudice, Sense and Sensibility, Emma, Mansfield Park, Persuasion, Lady Susan, Northanger Abbey

The Enheduanna cocktail, page 120

The Isabelle Eberhardt cocktail, page 94

ANNE BRONTË

1820 – 1849

We've always felt that Anne Brontë is unfairly underrated and neglected. Charlotte and Emily's novels are known the world over, but many people may not have even heard of Anne Brontë and still fewer have read any of her work. Brontë's lack of recognition is a shame, because her works deal openly with important societal themes, including her frank portrayal of the oppression of women. Both *Agnes Grey* and *The Tenant of Wildfell Hall* are blunt in their critique of women's positions in society.

Not all good cocktails need to be alcoholic. In deference to Anne Brontë's temperance views and beliefs in the dangers of alcohol, we have created for her a simple but refreshing non-alcoholic drink of sparkling lemonade and cucumber.

THE
ANNE BRONTË
COCKTAIL

Recipe
- 6 fl oz sparkling lemonade
- ¼ of a lime, freshly squeezed
- cucumber to garnish
- lime wedge to garnish

Pour lemonade over ice in a tall glass, add freshly squeezed lime juice. Garnish with cucumber slices and a lime wedge.

Notable works:
Agnes Grey, The Tenant of Wildfell Hall

MARY SHELLEY

1797 – 1851

Mary Shelley was the daughter of early feminist writer Mary Wollstonecraft, as well as a founder of the science-fiction genre. Her most famous work, *Frankenstein*, is a classic text that examines themes of science versus nature and ethics in science. Motherhood was also an important topic in her work as Shelley's mother died shortly after childbirth, and Shelley herself lost many children to miscarriage and illness. Shelley cited a nightmare as the origin of *Frankenstein*, which she told as a ghost story at the request of some friends during a party. She was then encouraged to draw the narrative out into a novel. At the time Shelley's husband, the poet Percy Bysshe Shelley, was thought to have exercised a great deal of conceptual and editorial power over the work, though she denied any major influence. In fact, it was Mary Shelley who, after her husband's death at the age of twenty-nine, took editorial control over his literary estate and reputation.

Muriel Spark cites Shelley as having said she could only perform in groups if she was slightly tipsy, and adds that Shelley would have lead a happier life if only she had drank more wine. Thus the Mary Shelley cocktail is a wine-based drink using rich, sweet port and high quality Scotch to give the cocktail an extra warmth and kick. We can imagine Shelley drinking this while curled up next to a roaring fire, scratching pen to paper during a storm as she fleshed out the tale that was to become one of science fiction's most classic and formative narratives, that of Frankenstein and his outcast creature.

THE
MARY SHELLEY
COCKTAIL

Recipe
– 1 ½ fl oz port
– 1 ½ fl oz scotch
– orange peel to garnish

In a cocktail shaker, pour port and scotch over ice and shake well. Strain into a chilled cocktail glass, and garnish with a twist of orange peel.

Notable works:
Frankenstein, The Last Man, Lodore, Falkner, Perkin Warbeck, Valperga

GEORGE ELIOT

1819 – 1880

A leading Victorian author, George Eliot was born in 1819 as Mary Ann Evans. After working as a successful critic and editor for some time, Eliot resolved to become a novelist. Desiring to be taken seriously and to avoid the misogynistic critiques leveled at female writers of the time, she adopted her masculine pen name prior to the publication of her first novel, *Adam Bede*, though her female identity was soon revealed. Her publicly acknowledged relationship with the married George Henry Lewes was also the cause of some scandal, but her popularity as a writer lead to her eventual acceptance back into polite society. This is not too surprising given the fact that Queen Victoria herself was a great admirer of Eliot's work. Her most famous novel is perhaps *Middlemarch*, described by Virginia Woolf as 'one of the few English novels written for grown-up people.' It is exemplary of her politically engaged realism, psychologically complex characters and astutely described rural settings.

When we think of Eliot, we think of elegance and subtlety. This drink is both of those things. Reminiscent of a calm summer's day in rural England, this non-alcoholic blend of apple and cardamom is sure to put those critics out of your mind.

THE
GEORGE ELIOT
COCKTAIL

Recipe
- 5 fl oz cloudy apple juice
- ½ fl oz fresh lemon juice
- ½ fl oz cardamom syrup
- lemon peel twist for garnish

Combine apple juice, lemon juice, and syrup. Pour over ice in a chilled Collins glass and add the lemon twist.

Notable works:
Adam Bede, Middlemarch, Silas Marner, Romola, Daniel Deronda, The Mill on the Floss

J.K. ROWLING

1965 – Present

J.K. Rowling is often dismissed as being 'just' a children's author. The Harry Potter series is one of the most famous sets of books worldwide and is hardly beloved only by children; the universal love of these books made Rowling richer than the Queen of England. Harry and his friends have captured the hearts of nearly every magic-lover in the world; grown adults still well up in tears at the merest mention of Fred Weasley, web games can sort you into your own Hogwarts House and some adventurous folks have formed their own skydiving Quidditch teams.

To remind you that Rowling's work is not just for children, we offer you an adult twist of the classic butterbeer: a blended butterscotch martini. Perfect for those summer evenings when you're visiting the lawn of Hogwarts!

THE
J.K. ROWLING
COCKTAIL

Recipe
- 1 cup vanilla ice cream
- 2 fl oz vodka
- 1 fl oz butterscotch schnapps

Combine ingredients in a blender until smooth and pour into a martini glass.

Notable works:
Harry Potter series, *The Casual Vacancy, The Cuckoo's Calling*

ZOË STRACHAN
1975 – Present

Zoë Strachan is a Scottish novelist, journalist, and university tutor who encouraged this project at its very conception. More than once, we have both burst into her office in full-fledged panic over our writing, and Strachan has calmly seen us through. Her voice, always soothing as she helps us untangle our work wherever we are stuck, is the best balm a PhD student could ask for. Strachan was born in Kilmarnock and currently teaches at the University of Glasgow.

We recommend all of Strachan's novels, but our favourite to date is her first, *Negative Space*. The novel is set primarily in Glasgow and ends in Orkney. It tells the story of a young narrator who is struggling through her grief at the death of her brother. Strachan's writing is straightforward and engaging; *Negative Space* is one of those novels that you read as you walk from the couch to the kettle, banging your knees into end tables because you can't tear your eyes from the page. Strachan writes with so much feeling, and her depiction of queer characters is invaluable to the literary world. Her characters' sexuality is never the focus of her work – they are not offered to the reader as 'the queer character'. Rather, they are (like queer folks in reality) simply people whose sexuality makes up one part of their complicated identity.

We asked Strachan what cocktail she would like, and she asked for a margarita. We had long been wanting to experiment with margarita recipes and were delighted to oblige. Here, then, is your Zoë Strachan cocktail – and, having had more than a few ourselves in the taste-testing process, we give it top marks. The raspberry herbal infusion blends nicely with the tequila to give you a tart, very drinkable margarita.

THE
ZOË STRACHAN
COCKTAIL

Recipe
- ½ cup raspberry herbal tea, strongly brewed
- 1 ½ fl oz tequila
- 1 fl oz triple sec
- Juice of ½ a lime
- fresh raspberries to garnish
- sugar or salt, to rim glasses

Rim margarita glass with sugar or salt. Shake raspberry tea, tequila, triple sec, and lime juice. Pour over a glass full of ice. Garnish with fresh raspberries.

Notable works:
Negative Space, Spin Cycle, Ever Fallen in Love

LOUISE WELSH

1965 – Present

Louise Welsh is a Glasgow-based author of short fiction and psychological thriller novels. Her work covers a wide variety of forms; she edited a book of ghost stories and wrote an opera, *The Devil Inside*, in collaboration with Scottish composer Stuart MacRae. The opera was born from Robert Louis Stevenson's short story 'The Bottle Imp'. If you're looking for a place to start with Welsh, we recommend *The Girl on the Stairs* for a compelling read on a chilly night. The book takes place in Berlin and explores motherhood, voyeurism, the relationship between two very different women and the effects of gaslighting and isolation on a woman in a new place.

Welsh's cocktail reflects the bloody nature of many of her books. A twist on the traditional Cape Cod, this cocktail features pomegranate juice and vodka with a slice of orange. The Louise Welsh looks tempting in the glass – a tiny pool of ruby-coloured liquid that shimmers under lamplight. This is also a wonderful cocktail for parties, as you can easily make it into a punch.

THE
LOUISE WELSH
COCKTAIL

Recipe
- 1 ½ fl oz vodka
- 3 fl oz pomegranate juice
- orange slices to garnish

Combine vodka and pomegranate juice, pour over ice into a glass. Garnish with an orange slice. This recipe also works well as a punch for parties. Simply add one part chilled vodka to three parts chilled pomegranate juice into a punch bowl and add orange slices to float on top.

As pomegranate juice can be expensive, opting for a pomegranate/apple (or other pomegranate juice blend) works equally well in this recipe.

Notable works:
The Devil Inside, The Girl on the Stairs, The Cutting Room, The Bullet Trick, Death is a Welcome Guest, Naming the Bones, Tamburlaine Must Die

ELIZABETH
BARRETT BROWNING
1806 – 1861

One of the Victorian period's most prolific and beloved poets, Elizabeth Barrett Browning is known for her *Sonnets from the Portuguese*, and her verse-novel *Aurora Leigh*. Born in 1806, she began writing as a child and went on to produce a large body of work, despite the poor health that would trouble her for the rest of her life. Due to her skill and popularity, she was considered for Poet Laureate in 1850 alongside Tennyson, who was granted the position. Though Barrett Browning is remembered for her love sonnets, much of her work was engaged with political and social issues. She wrote poems advocating against child labour and slavery, which deepened tensions with her father, whose fortune had been derived from slave labour in Jamaica. He would ultimately disinherit her after her secret courtship and marriage to fellow poet Robert Browning. In addition to her popularity in England, her writing had a great influence on American contemporaries such as Edgar Allen Poe and Emily Dickinson.

In our Elizabeth Barrett Browning cocktail, tart cranberry and citrus juices combine with warming cinnamon syrup to make a drink worthy of its namesake. We can't even begin to count the ways we adore this charming 'mocktail'.

THE
ELIZABETH BARRETT BROWNING COCKTAIL

Recipe
- 2 fl oz cranberry juice
- ½ fl oz lime juice
- ½ fl oz orange juice
- ½ fl oz cinnamon syrup
- lime twist to garnish

In a cocktail shaker, combine juices and syrup. Shake with ice and strain into a chilled lowball glass. Garnish with a twist of lime peel.

Notable works:
Sonnets from the Portuguese, Aurora Leigh, The Battle of Marathon

HOPE MIRRLEES

1887 – 1978

Hope Mirrlees was a modernist, a poet, a fantasy author, and a queer artist who stopped writing for decades after the death of her partner Jane Ellen Harrison. Hope Mirrlees has been all but erased and most of her work has fallen out-of-print, despite the exemplary quality of her writing. Her long poem, *Paris*, has been neglected by literary criticism, despite its striking similarity to T.S. Eliot's *The Wasteland*. Eliot's poem was written later and has thus created academic speculation that Eliot, who knew Mirrlees and her work, copied much of it for his own piece – which then received the critical acclaim that lasts today. Eliot himself wrote to Ezra Pound on the subject of women writers, saying, 'There are only half a dozen men of letters (and no women) worth printing'.

We couldn't disagree more. Mirrlees' fantasy novel *Lud-in-the-Mist* is among the finest novels ever written. Her prose is eloquent, witty, and complicated. In keeping with *Lud-in-the-Mist* tradition, we could do no less than give Mirrlees her own wild thyme gin cocktail. Here is a chance for you to expand your liquor infusion skills and create a unique martini that truly deserves its name.

THE
HOPE MIRRLEES COCKTAIL

Recipe
- 1 part vermouth
- 5 parts thyme-infused gin
- ice
- sprig of thyme to garnish

Shake 1 part vermouth with 5 parts thyme-infused gin and ice. Strain into martini glass and garnish with a sprig of thyme.

Beware! This cocktail tastes like a very, very dirty martini.

Notable works:
Paris, The Counterplot, Lud-in-the-Mist

DOROTHY WORDSWORTH

1771 – 1855

Until recently, Dorothy Wordsworth was known primarily as the sister of famous Romantic poet William Wordsworth, but with the rise of feminist literary criticism her skill as a poet and diarist, and her influence on William's work, has come to light. Born in 1771, Wordsworth lived in a time unsupportive of women writers and had no desire to become a published writer herself. Instead, she devoted her energies to supporting her brother's literary career, acting as a sort of secretary for him and going so far as to gather material for his poems, which she would record in her journals. The most famous example of this is her poetic account of seeing daffodils near Lake Grasmere, which her brother lifted for one of his most famous poems, 'Daffodils', written two years later. Similarly, he used her account of climbing Scafell Pike to write his guidebook to the Lake District. Unsurprisingly, he did not credit her for such contributions to his work, though his success as a writer was hugely dependent on her support and that of his wife and daughter. Fortunately, she is now recognized as a writer whose talents equal, if not surpass, those of her brother. Her *Grasmere Journal* in particular is a beautifully written record of her life in the Lake District. Towards the end of her life, Wordsworth grew increasingly ill and bed-ridden, partially as the result of an opiate addiction from taking laudanum. She died in 1855.

Thinking of Wordsworth's long, chilly walks in the countryside, we have made her drink a restorative Hot Toddy. There are many variations out there, but trust us: this is the perfect ratio of whisky, lemon, and honey to warm your hands and heart.

THE
DOROTHY WORDSWORTH COCKTAIL

Recipe
– 1 ½ fl oz whisky
– juice of half a lemon
– 2 tbsp honey
– hot water
– cinnamon stick
– lemon slice with cloves

In a mug, combine the whisky and lemon juice. Fill with hot water, stir in the honey, and add a cinnamon stick. If you like cloves in your hot toddies, we recommend studding them into the rind of a lemon slice to keep them under control. Toss it in last, and enjoy.

Notable works:
Grasmere Journal, Home at Grasmere

DORIS LESSING

1919 – 2013

Our favourite Doris Lessing moment was when reporters came to tell her she had won the Nobel Prize and she more or less told them to scat and get off her lawn.

Lessing was one of the most important writers of British literature. Even if you have never read her, you've surely heard of her work: *The Golden Notebook*, *Memoirs of a Survivor*, *The Cleft* – many of these can be found on the shelves of English literature scholars worldwide. Lessing's strength as a writer in that she wrote fluidly between realism, magical realism and fantasy without a single care for the literary hierarchy of genre fiction. Lessing, like many of the women here, was a feminist who refused to apologise for her life choices. If you haven't read her yet, we recommend starting with *The Fifth Child*, a chilling and heart-wrenching look into one of the worst-case scenarios of motherhood.

To do justice to Lessing's admirable character, we present you with a spin on the Salty Dog – a gin and grapefruit cocktail seared with sea salt and a twist of lime for that extra sour pinch at your lips.

THE
DORIS LESSING COCKTAIL

Recipe
- 1 ½ fl oz gin
- 2 fl oz grapefruit juice
- wedge of lime
- saltwater (dissolve coarse sea salt into boiling water, cool) to taste

Shake gin, grapefruit juice and saltwater with ice until very cold. Pour into a glass and squeeze in a wedge of lime.

Notable works:
The Golden Notebook, Memoirs of a Survivor, The Cleft, The Fifth Child

ZADIE SMITH
1975 – Present

One of England's most popular living novelists, Zadie Smith was born in London to a Jamaican mother and English father. In circumstances that garnered great publicity, the 21-year-old Smith's incomplete first novel was picked up after a bidding war between several publishers while she was still studying at Cambridge University. The comedic and expansive *White Teeth* was an instant commercial and critical success, cementing Smith's reputation as a rising literary star. The novel follows three London families from diverse ethnic backgrounds and examines, amongst other things, the impact of immigration on cultural identity. Smith's second novel, *The Autograph Man*, and her third, *On Beauty*, have likewise been successful, with the latter being shortlisted for the Man Booker Prize, and winning the 2006 Orange Prize for Fiction and Commonwealth Writer's Best Book Award. Smith's recent novel, *NW*, is her most daring yet, bringing together a multitude of narrative techniques to reflect the socioeconomic discord of contemporary London life. In 2002 she was elected a fellow of the Royal Society of Literature.

Paralleling the zing of postmodern irony so characteristic of Smith's work, this tart cocktail is a take on the classic Brown Derby, substituting tequila for bourbon.

THE
ZADIE SMITH
COCKTAIL

Recipe
- 1 ½ fl oz tequila
- 1 fl oz fresh
  grapefruit juice
- ½ fl oz honey syrup

For the honey syrup, dissolve honey into an equal part of hot water.

In a cocktail shaker, combine tequila, juice, and honey syrup. Shake with ice and strain into a chilled martini glass.

Notable works:
White Teeth, *The Autograph Man* , *On Beauty*, NW

BEATRIX POTTER

1866 – 1943

Women who write children's books are rarely taken seriously as authors, which we find a shame. There's an argument to be made that the skills needed for writing a children's book are even more complex than writing a book for adults: children's writing requires the ability to speak to children at their level without being patronising or simplistic – a type of code-switching that needs a fine balance. Beatrix Potter struck a beautiful balance with her lovely stories about animals. When we think back to our favorite childhood reading experiences, Peter Rabbit and Jeminia Puddleduck are strong figures in our memories. Potter's iconic illustrations of her characters are cherished by children and adults worldwide.

Potter was not only an author and illustrator, she was a complex, fascinating woman with a strong taste for nature and its conservation. For her cocktail, we have looked to both her pages and her gardens for inspiration. There is perhaps no better match for our love of home-infused liquors; therefore, we offer you a blackberry-soaked cocktail that will bring the heady taste of early autumn into your glasses. Inhale deeply as you sip this botanical cocktail and remember the love of nature you received as a child from Beatrix Potter's tales.

THE
BEATRIX POTTER COCKTAIL

Recipe
- 1 ½ fl oz blackberry vodka (infuse a handful of blackberries in vodka in an airtight container for 3–5 days)
- 2 fl oz sparkling lemonade
- 1 tsp honey syrup
- fresh mint

In a cocktail shaker, combine the gin and honey syrup. Shake with ice, strain into a Mason jar, and add the sparkling lemonade. Garnish with a blackberry and a sprig of mint.

Notable works:
The Tale of Peter Rabbit, The Tale of Tom Kitten, The Tale of Mrs Tiggy-Winkle, The Tale of Jemima Puddle-Duck

EUROPE

SIMONE DE BEAUVOIR

1908 – 1986

French writer and intellectual Simone de Beauvoir is best known for her classic work of feminist philosophy *The Second Sex*, published in 1949. This foundational second-wave text addresses the history of women's oppression and contains her famous statement on gender performativity, that 'one is not born, but rather becomes, a woman.' Born in 1908 into a bourgeois family, de Beauvoir rebelled against the gender and class expectations of her time to pursue a life of intellectualism, an experience recounted in her 1958 autobiography *Memoirs of a Dutiful Daughter*. It also recalls her early days with existential philosopher Jean-Paul Sartre, with whom she would have a lifelong relationship. Although she is known for her critical theory, de Beauvoir also wrote novels, including *She Came to Stay* and *The Mandarins*, for which she won the 1954 Prix Goncourt.

The next time you're sitting down for some serious feminist philosophising, grab a brandy snifter and arm yourself with this elegant cocktail. The Simone de Beauvoir cocktail is a rich blend of brandy and port, with cinnamon syrup for a touch of spice and lemon juice for bite.

THE
SIMONE DE BEAUVOIR COCKTAIL

Recipe
- 1 fl oz brandy
- 1 fl oz port
- ½ fl oz honey cinnamon syrup
- ¼ fl oz lemon juice
- lemon peel twist to garnish

For the syrup, combine equal parts honey and water on the stovetop and add a cinnamon stick. Heat while stirring until the honey is dissolved and the mixture tastes strongly of cinnamon. Store the excess in the fridge.

In a cocktail shaker, combine the brandy, port, syrup, and lemon juice. Shake with ice, and strain into a chilled brandy snifter. Garnish with a twist of lemon peel.

Notable works:
The Second Sex, Memoirs of a Dutiful Daughter, She Came to Stay, The Mandarins, The Broken Woman, A Very Easy Death

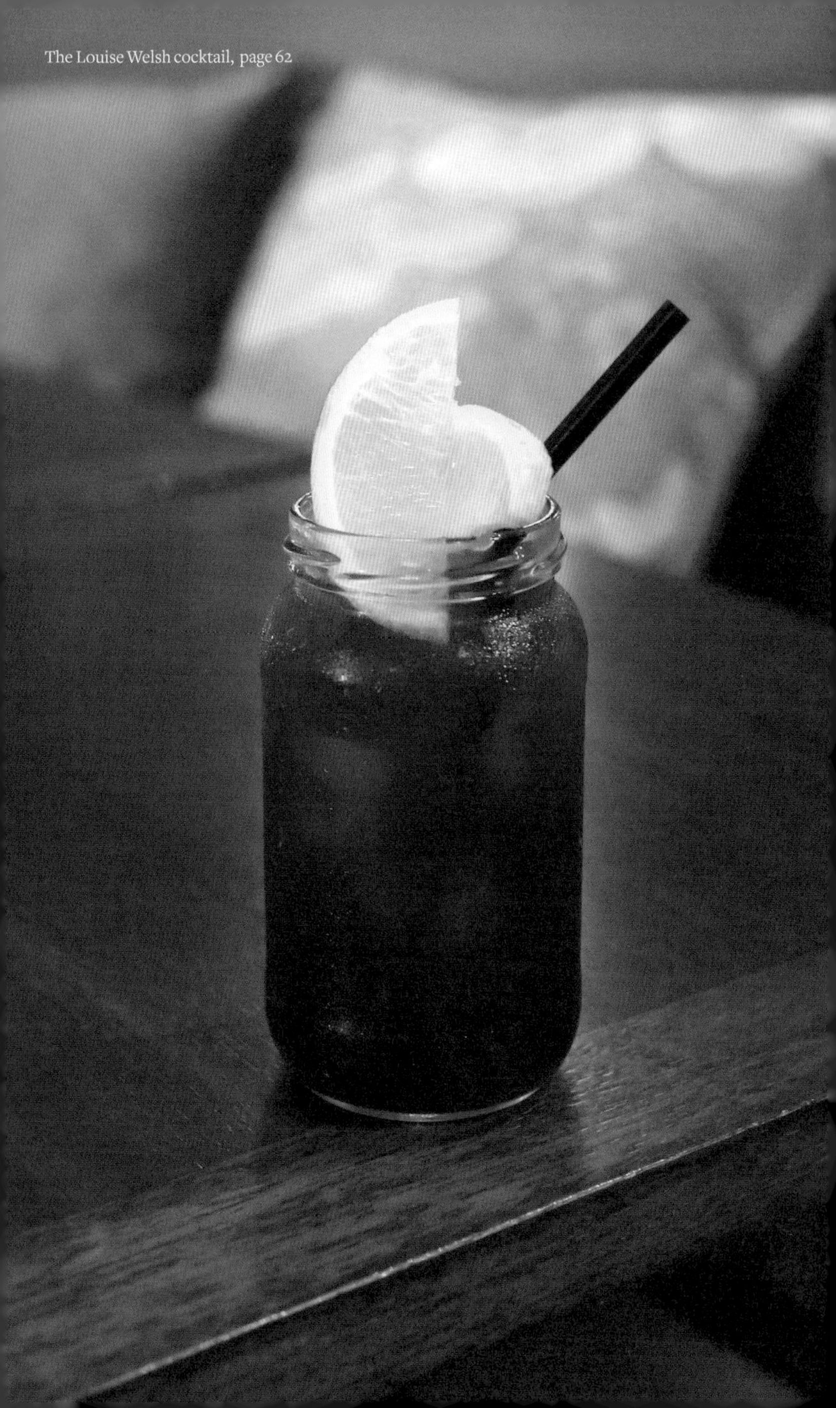

The Louise Welsh cocktail, page 62

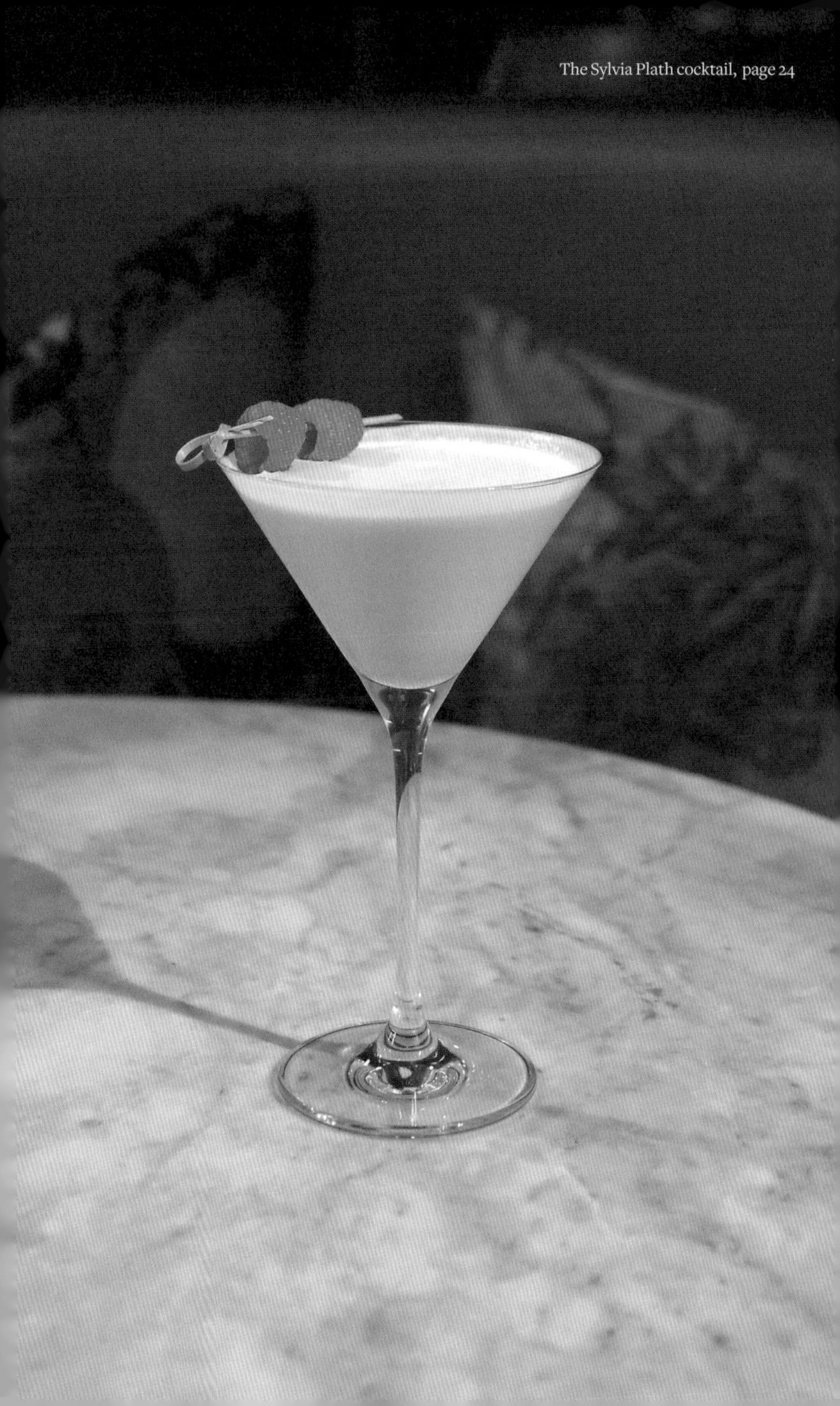

The Sylvia Plath cocktail, page 24

MARGUERITE DURAS

1914 – 1996

Born in former Saigon to French parents at the beginning of the 20th century, Marguerite Duras is a French writer best known for her novels and screenplays. The 1984 Prix Goncourt-winning *L'Amant* is an autobiographical account of Duras' youth in Indochina; it details the abuse she suffered at the hands of her mother and older brother and the class and racial tensions underpinning her adolescent affair with a wealthy and much older Chinese man, Huynh Thuy Le. At the age of 17, Duras moved to France to pursue an education, studying first mathematics, then political science, after which she became an active member of the French Communist Party. She was also a member of the French Resistance during the Second World War. Her prolific literary output began in 1943 with the publication of her first novel, *Les Impudents*. The form of both her novels and screenplays became increasingly experimental, but nonetheless remained commercially successful. Her screenplay for the 1959 film *Hiroshima mon amour*, now considered a foundation of French New Wave cinema, brought her fame and an Academy Award nomination for Best Original Screenplay.

With a daring blend of dark rum, cloudy lemonade, and the liquorice flavour of absinthe, our Marguerite Duras cocktail is a unique tribute to this French literary icon.

THE
MARGUERITE DURAS COCKTAIL

Recipe
- 1 ½ fl oz dark rum
- ¼ fl oz absinthe substitute
- 3 fl oz cloudy lemonade

Combine ingredients and pour over ice in a chilled lowball glass.

Notable works:
L'Amant, Les Impudents, Un Barrage contre le Pacifique, Moderato Cantabile, Hiroshima mon amour

GEORGE SAND

1804 – 1876

Born in 1804 as Amantine-Lucile-Aurore Dupin, this French Romantic novelist is better known by her pen name George Sand, adopted early in her literary career for her first novel, *Indiana*. In that work and others, she protested the legal and social restrictions that limited human relationships, a theme of personal significance in her own life. After separating from her husband, with great detriment to her social reputation, Sand had many scandalous affairs, including those with dramatist Alfred de Musset and composer Frédéric Chopin. She was also notorious for smoking and wearing men's clothing in public, which allowed her a freedom of movement denied to women of the time. She and her work were greatly admired by contemporaries such as Gustave Flaubert and Honoré de Balzac, and she was also a politically engaged critic with socialist views, supporting the working class and women's rights.

With its sweet blend of peach and amaretto, and lemon juice for a splash of personality, this is the perfect cocktail to honour our favorite trouser-wearing 19th century lady.

THE
GEORGE SAND
COCKTAIL

Recipe
- ¾ fl oz amaretto
- 1 fl oz white rum
- 1 fl oz peach juice
- 1 tsp lemon juice
- slice of peach to
  garnish

In a cocktail shaker, combine amaretto, rum, peach and lemon juice. Shake with ice and strain into a chilled martini glass. Garnish with a slice of peach.

Notable works:
La Mare au Diable, Indiana, La Petite Fadette, Consuelo, Lélia, Mauprat, François le Champi

FRANÇOISE SAGAN

1935 – 2004

When *Bonjour Tristesse* was published in 1954, eighteen-year-old Françoise Sagan became an instant literary celebrity. Critically acclaimed, yet surrounded by controversy, her first novel daringly explored the sexuality of its teenage heroine, Cécile, as she vacationed in the French Riviera. In a style of misogyny thought to have died with the 19th century, rumours briefly circulated that an older, male author had written the book and was using the cover of a teenage girl to generate scandal. Regardless, Sagan spent her fortune drinking, gambling and driving sports cars, and was undoubtedly the wild child of mid-20th century French literature. She would go on to write many novels, plays, song lyrics and screenplays.

We vote Sagan 'most likely to drink you under the table', so to honour her we've put a twist on the strongest drink we could think of: the Long Island Iced Tea. All the alcohol you have in your liquor cabinet, plus some absinthe to really kick the legs out from under you.

THE
FRANÇOISE SAGAN COCKTAIL

Recipe
- ½ fl oz vodka
- ½ fl oz whiksy
- ½ fl oz white rum
- ½ fl oz tequila
- ¼ fl oz absinthe
- juice of half a lemon
- splash of cola

In a Collins glass, combine the vodka, whisky, rum, tequila, absinthe, and lemon juice. Add ice, and top with a splash of cola.

Notable works:
Bonjour Tristesse, A Certain Smile, Aimez-vous Brahms?, La Chamade

CHRISTA WOLF

1929 – 2011

Christa Wolf is one of the most famous German authors, critics, and essayists of the 20th century. She was an East German writer who focused heavily on feminism and socialism in her work. One of Wolf's most famous books is *Cassandra*, a re-telling of the Trojan War from the perspective of Cassandra, the ill-fated prophetic daughter of King Priam. *Medea*, another Wolf novel, re-imagines the gruesome tale of Medea with feminist compassion. Both novels offer a new perspective on matriarchy, feminine power, and the realities and truths of iconic female characters in old Greek myths. Wolf's writing is rich in politics and societal commentary, making her one of the most important German writers in recent memory.

When we think of Christa Wolf, we think of her sitting at a desk stacked full of papers, with pieces of novels and essays surrounding her typewriter. The best companion we know for working long hours at one's desk is a hot cup of coffee, and we bet many Germans would agree with us. Therefore, the Christa Wolf is a rich cocktail consisting of strong coffee with the accompanying satisfaction of hazelnut liqueur. Enjoy it hot or iced, according to your mood (and the weather).

THE
CHRISTA WOLF
COCKTAIL

Recipe
- 6 fl oz hot, strong coffee
- 1 fl oz hazelnut liqueur
- milk or cream

Add hazelnut liqueur to coffee and stir. Add milk or cream and serve in warm mugs. Alternatively, use iced coffee for a chilled version of this cocktail.

Notable works:
Cassandra, Medea, Der geteilte Himmel, The Quest for Christa T., Patterns of Childhood

HERTA MÜLLER

1953 – Present

Herta Müller, a Romanian-born German writer, was the 2009 recipient of the Nobel Prize for Literature. She writes novels, poetry and essays, and her work primarily focuses on the perspectives of the German minority in Romania and other places. The Swedish Academy described her as a writer 'who, with the concentration of poetry and the frankness of prose, depicts the landscape of the dispossessed'.

Müller wrote from a place of trauma, oppression and violence; out of tragedy and pain comes much of humanity's greatest works. We admire women who write about the most bitter of subjects with the aim of shedding light on dark places; such writing forms its own particular beauty.

The Herta Müller cocktail can be made with white rum or vodka. Müller was born in a very rural village, which evokes thoughts of wildflowers and herbs – as well as all the tasty treats that can be made with them. Lavender-infused liquor mixes well with lemon and simple syrup to make a homemade lemonade and lavender cocktail that will give you a taste of the countryside.

THE
HERTA MÜLLER COCKTAIL

Recipe
- 2 fl oz lavender-
  infused white rum
- 4 fl oz fresh lemonade
  (not sparkling)
- lavender simple syrup
  to taste
- lavender sugar
  (optional)

To make lavender sugar, combine fresh, chopped lavender flowers in a small jar of white sugar. Store for 2–3 days before using.

Mix lavender-infused white rum, lemon juice, and simple syrup into a cocktail shaker and add ice. Shake until very cold, then pour into martini glasses rimmed with lavender sugar (if desired). Garnish with sprig of lavender and/or a slice of lemon.

For an iced tea version of this cocktail, try adding 2 fl oz lavender rum, the juice of ½ a lemon, 2 tablespoons of Cointreau, and a pinch of lavender sugar to a glass of Earl Grey iced tea.

Notable works:
The Passport, The Land of Green Plums, The Appointment, The Hunger Angel

DOROTHEA VIEHMANN

1755 – 1815

Many will not have heard of Dorothea Viehmann, but all of you know her work. Viehmann was the daughter of a German tavern owner and was born near Kassel, now widely recognised as the fairy tale capital of the world. Viehmann was a storyteller and the source of many of Jacob and Wilhelm Grimm's fairy tales. Viehmann is an important figure in this cocktail book because she represents what so many of us in history have faced – her own work credited to two male academics. The Grimms are remembered by scholars, children, parents and fantasy lovers alike, but few remember that there was a woman storyteller and her oral folk tales behind the iconic works.

For Viehmann, we have created a fairy tale cocktail for you. Because she is German, we opted for apple schnapps. Mixed with spicy ginger and a kick of brandy, this cocktail will taste like a grown-up version of Snow White's forbidden apple.

THE
DOROTHEA VIEHMANN
COCKTAIL

Recipe
- 2 fl oz apple schnapps
- 3 fl oz ginger cordial
- 1 fl oz brandy
- cinnamon sticks, fresh ginger, apple slices to garnish (optional)
- vanilla bean to garnish (optional)

Mix schnapps, cordial and brandy. Pour into a glass over ice and garnish with a cinnamon stick, fresh ginger, apple slice, and/or vanilla bean if desired.

Note: If you're having trouble locating ginger cordial, try using ginger beer instead and adding a ginger simple syrup to taste.

Notable works:
The Twelve Brothers, The Little Peasant, The Goose Girl, The Peasant's Wise Daughter, The Iron Stove

ISABELLE EBERHARDT

1877 – 1904

Late-19th century writer and explorer Isabelle Eberhardt is little known today, despite her radical and fascinating life. Born in Switzerland in 1877 to an Armenian ex-priest father and an aristocratic Russian mother, Eberhardt reaped the benefit of her father's anarchic political views when he raised her with a son's education and freedom. She spent much of her short life travelling North Africa in the guise of a man, working as a correspondent for a French newspaper. There, she converted to Islam, and wrote passionately about the faith in her books and journals, considering it her life's deepest calling. At the age of twenty-seven, Eberhardt died in a flash flood in Algeria where she was living with her husband, who recovered her journals and papers from the wreckage of their house.

In honour of this free-spirited adventurer we have chosen a variation of the classic Aviation cocktail, with orange blossom water as a substitute for Creme de Violette to give it a North African twist.

THE

ISABELLE EBERHARDT
COCKTAIL

Recipe
- 2 fl oz gin
- ½ fl oz lime juice
- ¾ fl oz honey syrup
- 2–3 dashes orange
  blossom water
- lime slice to garnish

In a cocktail shaker, combine gin, lime juice, honey syrup, and orange blossom water. Shake with ice and strain into a chilled cocktail glass. Garnish with a slice of lime.

Notable works:
The Oblivion Seekers, The Nomad, Prisoner of Dunes, In the Shadow of Islam

TOVE JANSSON

1914 – 2001

Tove Jansson was a Finnish writer, painter and illustrator, born in 1914 to artistic parents who would have a great influence on her career. She is best known for writing and illustrating her beloved Moomin books, which chronicle the adventures of a carefree family of round, white, snouted troll creatures. Though the Moomins have their origin in Jansson's childhood, they entered the world at large with the 1945 publication of *The Moomins and the Great Flood*, and gained fame with the subsequent *Comet in Moominland* and *Finn Family Moomintroll*. The books display political undertones and psychological depth beneath their outward charm, dealing with the repercussions of the Second World War and themes of homosexuality. In 1956 Jansson met the woman with whom she would share her life and work, Tuulikki Pietilä, an influential graphic artist. Pietilä featured in *Moominland Midwinter* as the character Too-Ticky.

Jansson ultimately focused her attention on writing for adults, beginning with *Sculptor's Daughter* in 1968 and would go on to produce many novels and short story collections. Jansson received the Hans Christian Andersen Award for children's literature in 1966.

In the spirit of her Moomin books, the Tove Jansson cocktail is a charming pink lemonade: sweet and fun, with a serious amount of whisky beneath.

THE
TOVE JANSSON COCKTAIL

Recipe
- 6 fl oz cloudy lemonade
- 2 fl oz whisky
- 1 tsp grenadine
- 1 lemon slice to garnish

Combine lemonade, whisky, and grenadine. Pour over ice in a Collins glass, and top with a lemon slice for garnish.

Notable works:
The Moomins books, *The Summer Book*, *The True Deceiver*

KAREN BLIXEN

1885 – 1962

You might know this Danish author better as Isak Dinesen, the pen name under which she wrote her most famous book, *Out of Africa*. Published in 1937, this lyrical memoir chronicles the seventeen years Blixen spent on her coffee plantation in Kenya, and provides an insightful, if sometimes disturbing, personal record of colonial influence in the area. She also wrote fiction, and is well known for *Seven Gothic Tales* and her story *Babette's Feast*, which like *Out of Africa* was adapted into an Academy Award-winning film. Blixen began publishing fiction at an early age, but didn't become serious about it until she returned to Denmark in the early 1930s. She usually wrote first in English, before translating her own work into Danish, and despite her somewhat old-fashioned writing style, was admired by contemporaries such as Ernest Hemingway and Truman Capote. Blixen was considered for the 1962 Nobel Prize in Literature, but became ineligible when she died that year.

As a reference to Blixen's beloved coffee plantation, we've created a drink that skips the coffee liqueur and goes straight for the real thing. A cool blend of espresso, vodka, amaretto and cream, this caffeinated cocktail is a perfect tribute to this Danish author.

THE
KAREN BLIXEN
COCKTAIL

Recipe
- 1 fl oz cold espresso
- 1 fl oz vodka
- ½ fl oz amaretto
- 1 ½ tbsp cream
- twist of orange peel
  to garnish

In a cocktail shaker, combine espresso, vodka, amaretto and cream. Shake with ice and strain into a chilled lowball glass. Run an a twist of orange peel along the rim and toss in for garnish.

Notable works:
Out of Africa, Seven Gothic Tales, Babette's Feast, Shadows on the Grass, Anecdotes of Destiny

SAPPHO

630 – 570 BCE

Sappho was born sometime around 630 BCE on the Greek island of Lesbos. Her poetry spoke so movingly about romantic love and relationships between women that her birthplace, Lesbos, became the root word of 'lesbian'. While much of Sappho's work has been lost, fragments of her poetry remain. Her versus are filled with light, like a prism held up to the window to catch sunbeams.

With a poet like Sappho, nothing but honey mead would do for a recipe. Sappho's work reminds us of honey – clear but sweet – and her poems frequently speak of pleasure and the senses, including food and dance and celebration. Mead is like her poetry in drink form. Think of Sappho when you drink her cocktail and we recommend treating yourself to a copy of Anne Carson's *If not, winter: fragments of Sappho* for the occasion.

THE
SAPPHO COCKTAIL

Recipe
- 2 parts chilled mead (honey wine)
- 1 part chilled orange juice
- splash of soda water or sparkling wine, for fizz
- orange peel, to garnish

Add mead and orange juice to a champagne flute, stir. Splash soda water or sparkling wine overtop for a bit of fizz. Garnish with a curl of orange peel.

Optional: A splash of bourbon to each glass gives an extra kick to this elegant drink.

Notable works:
If not, winter, The Love Songs of Sappho, The Poetry of Sappho

REST OF THE WORLD

ANNA AKHMATOVA
1889 – 1996

This acclaimed Russian poet was born Anna Andreyevna Gorenko in 1889. When her father forbade her to publish under the family name, she adopted 'Akhmatova' for a pen name, after her maternal grandmother. Her first collection, *Evening*, was published in 1912 to great success, and her second book, *Rosary*, followed two years later, securing her literary reputation. Along with her first husband, Nikolay Gumilev, Akhmatova was a major figure in the Acmeist poetic movement, which valued clarity and craft in contrast to the vague Symbolist style then fashionable. This period of writing took place in what is considered the Silver Age of Russian poetry, the end of which was marked in part by Gumilev's execution by the Soviet secret police in 1921. Because of Akhmatova's affiliation with him, she was prevented from publishing for many years, but she stayed in Russia to bear witness to the political events happening around her, including the death of her partner Nikolai Punin and the imprisonment of her son. During this time she composed her most famous work, *Requiem*, a reaction to the Stalinist terror.

Don't be deceived by its sweet and nutty taste: this cocktail is not for the weak of heart. With three fluid ounces of undiluted alcohol, one could even call it Acmeist in its directness. You might recognize the combination of vodka, gin, and crème de cacao as a type of Black Russian, but we've added a hint of Frangelico to make this drink as unique as Akhmatova.

THE
ANNA AKHMATOVA
COCKTAIL

Recipe
- 1 fl oz vodka
- 1 fl oz gin
- ¾ fl oz crème de cacao
- ¼ fl oz Frangelico

Combine ingredients and pour into a chilled lowball glass over ice.

Notable works:
Evening, Rosary, Requiem, You Will Hear Thunder

The Toni Morrison cocktail, page 4

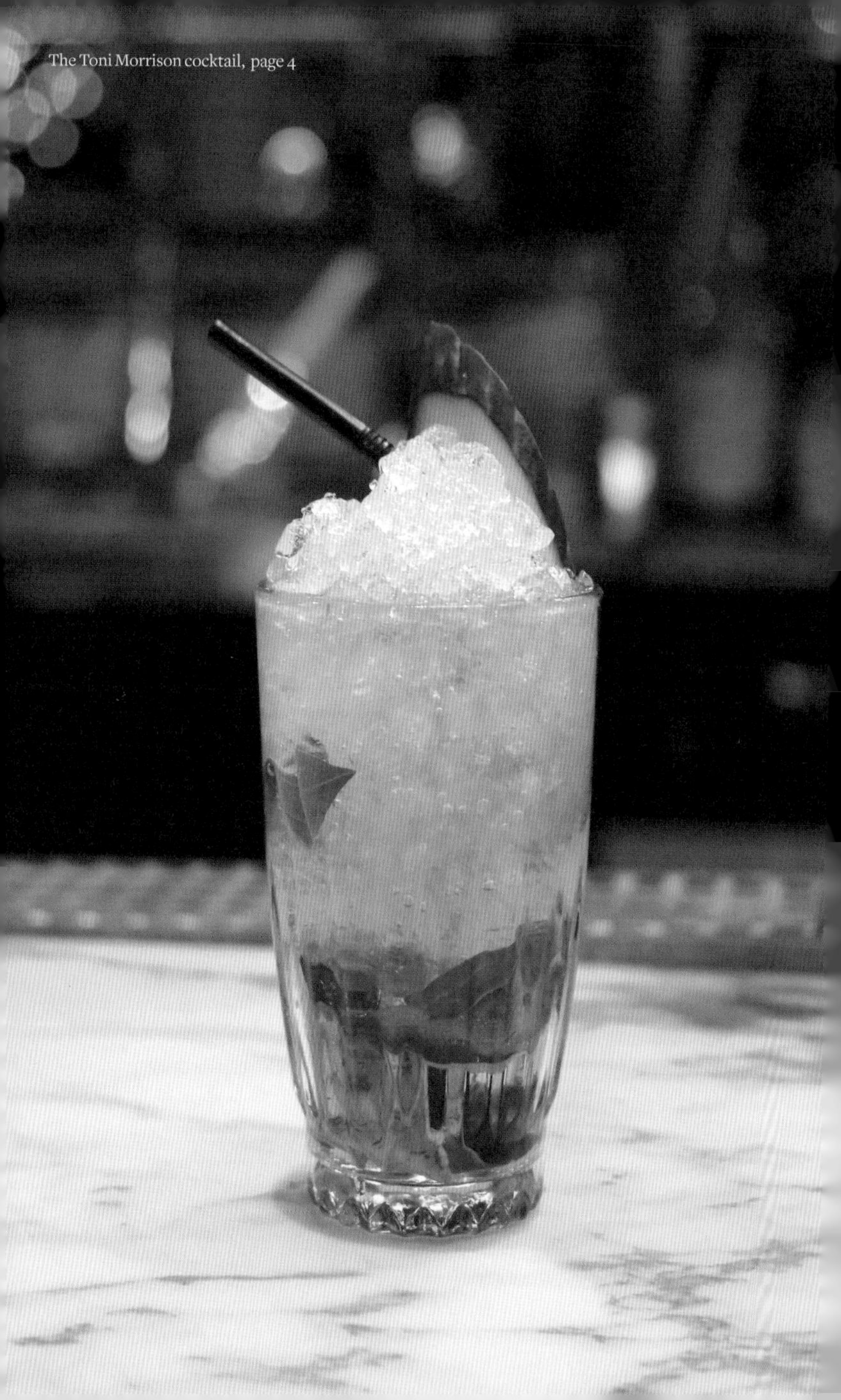

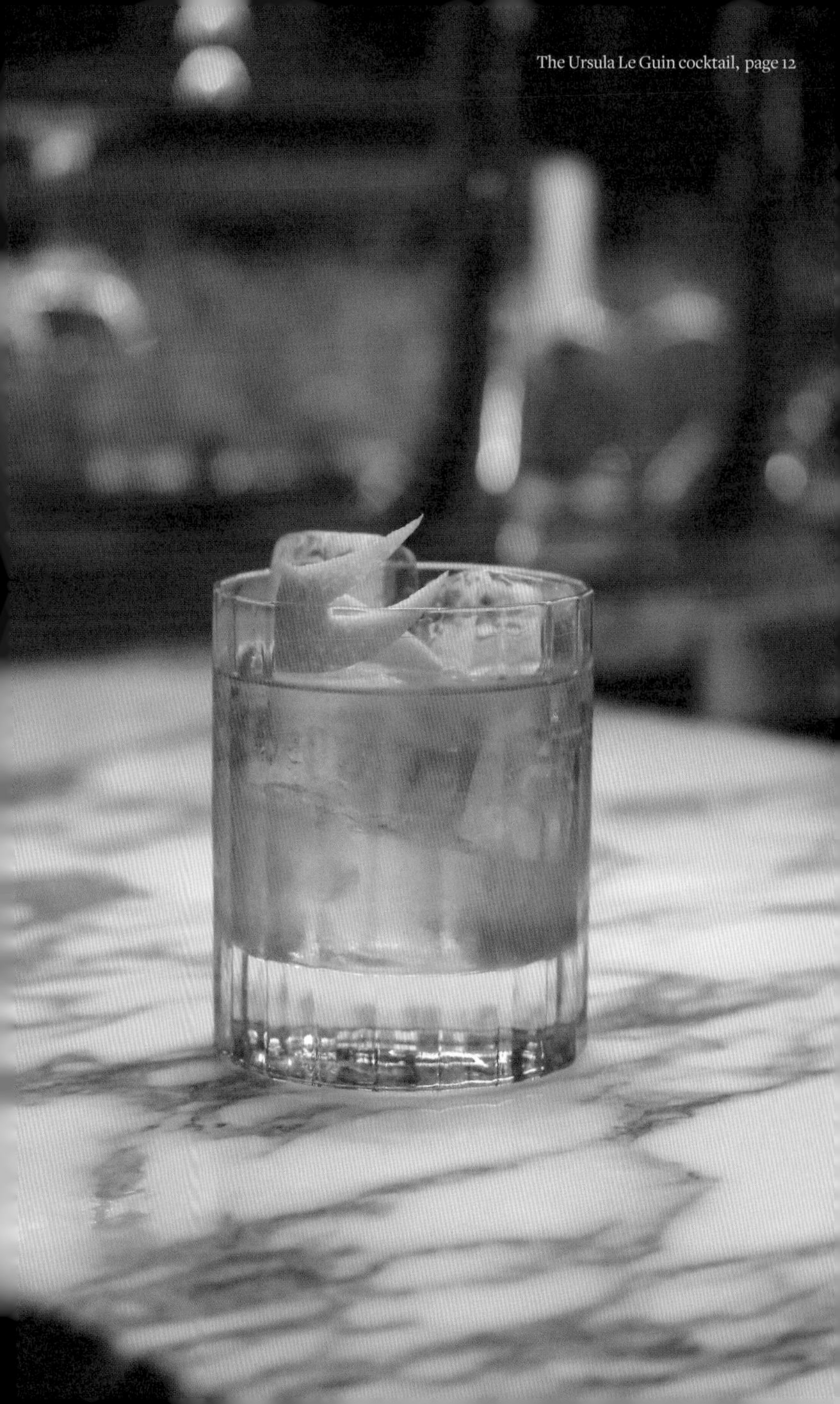

The Ursula Le Guin cocktail, page 12

MURASAKI SHIKIBU

973 AD

Murasaki Shikibu is the nickname of the unknown author of *The Tale of Genji*, a Japanese novel written around the year 1,000. She also wrote a collection of poetry called *The Diary of Lady Murasaki*. The names of women were not recorded during this period of history, so we only have a nickname to remember her by. Shikibu was a novelist, poet and lady-in-waiting. *The Tale of Genji* is often called the world's first modern novel.

We adore the fact that a woman was the author of the world's first novel. Men have dominated the literary scene for so long and continue to do so; women's ability to write at all has been and still is questioned frequently in literary circles. The erasure of women, the devaluation of our work, our exclusion from literary circles, the publishing discrimination we face, the sexism in marketing and interviewing, the way our work is taught in schools – this and so much more, seems even more ridiculous when you consider that a woman is generally credited with the construction of the first novel.

Shikibu's cocktail is a saketini, a contemporary cocktail for a classic woman. This recipe asks you to make plum vodka, but you could easily substitute in another fruit.

THE
MURASAKI SHIKIBU COCKTAIL

Recipe
- 1 part sake
- 1 part plum-infused vodka
- plum slices to garnish
- fresh ginger slices to garnish (optional)

Shake sake and vodka with ice until very cold, strain into martini glass. Garnish with a slender plum slice and/or slices of fresh ginger.

This recipe is ideal for experimenting with your vodka infusions. Consider trying cucumber, white peach, cherry, apple, or pear for a different taste.

Notable works:
The Tale of Genji, The Diary of Lady Murasaki, Poetic Memoirs

MILES FRANKLIN

1879 – 1954

Miles Franklin is one of Australia's most well known writers. Her rebellious 1901 novel *My Brilliant Career*, about an ambitious girl growing up in rural New South Wales, was her great literary achievement. Following its publication, she moved in feminist circles while living in Sydney and Melbourne, but in 1906 moved to the United States where she worked for the National Women's Trade Union League. During this time she chose never to marry because of the limitations it would inflict upon her. Later she lived in England for a number of years, leaving briefly to volunteer for the Scottish Women's Hospitals for Foreign Service in Macedonia during the First World War. Upon returning to Australia she wrote several novels under the pseudonym Brent of Bin Bin, wanting to distance herself from the popularity and pressures of her first book.

Franklin was instrumental in fostering the development of Australian literature by encouraging young writers and literary publications and creating the Miles Franklin Award promoting literature about Australian life. In 2013, the Stella Prize for Australian women writers was established, referencing Franklin, whose given name was 'Stella'.

For our Miles Franklin cocktail we've combined mango juice, cream, and a rebellious dose of coconut rum to create a smooth and delicious cocktail. It's the perfect drink to have in hand while appreciating this author's brilliant career.

THE
MILES FRANKLIN
COCKTAIL

Recipe
– 1 ½ fl oz coconut rum
– 2 fl oz mango juice
– 1 tbsp cream

Combine ingredients in a cocktail shaker and shake with ice. Strain into a chilled martini glass and enjoy.

Notable works:
My Brilliant Career, Some Everyday Folk and Dawn, Old Blastus of Bandicoot, Pioneers on Parade

ARUNDHATI ROY
1961 – Present

Indian novelist Arundhati Roy is best known for her only published novel, the 1997 Man Booker Prize-winning *The God of Small Things*. The book recounts the lives of fraternal twins growing up in Kerala, India, in the 1960s and meeting later in the 1990s. Reflecting Roy's dedication to social justice, the novel examines Indian political tensions, past and present, through the deeply personal effects they have on her characters: the social discrimination of India's caste system and the repercussions of colonialism are among her many themes. Stylistically, the novel's non-sequential narrative and shifting viewpoints masterfully depict the process of remembering trauma and serve to emphasize the crossing-points of personal and political history. And let's not forget to mention Roy's many female characters, who bolster the book with their strength and complexity.

Previously, Roy worked as a screenwriter, and has continued to do so since writing her novel. She has also written a truly prolific number of articles and essays on a wide range of social issues. Her commitment to political and social activism resulted in her being awarded the Sydney Peace Prize in 2004.

For our Arundhati Roy cocktail, we have created a unique mojito. With refreshing mint-infused rum and colorful slices of mango, this is a drink worthy of Roy's vivid and lyrical prose style.

THE
ARUNDHATI ROY COCKTAIL

Recipe
- 2 fl oz mint-infused white rum
- 1 fl oz fresh lime juice
- 2 tsp caster sugar
- 1 splash soda water
- 12 fresh mint leaves
- 4–5 slices raw mango

Muddle mango, mint, and sugar in a Collins glass. Add ice. Pour over rum, add a splash of soda water, and stir.

This recipe works with other fruits as well. Strawberry or any type of melon are great alternatives. Additionally, flavoured simple syrups – such as lavender, lemon, or orange – make for other great twists on the mojito. And if you don't like rum, consider using gin!

Notable works:
The God of Small Things, Capitalism: A Ghost Story

TSITSI DANGAREMBGA

1959 – Present

Born in 1959, Tsitsi Dangarembga is a Zimbabwean writer and filmmaker known for her novel *Nervous Conditions*. Published in 1988 to critical acclaim, this semi-autobiographical book won the Commonwealth Writers' Prize and has become a classic of African feminism and postcolonial literature. It follows a girl growing up in 1960s Rhodesia, determined to pursue an education in the face patriarchal oppression, yet dealing with the cultural consequences of that education, which threatens to divide her from her family and heritage. This was a familiar situation for Dangarambga, who herself began her education as a child in England, and later studied medicine at Cambridge University. Dangarembga has since turned to film as a medium. She wrote the story for the 1993 film *Neria*, the highest-grossing film in Zimbabwean history, and directed the 1996 *Everyone's Child*, becoming the first black Zimbabwean woman to direct a feature film.

Dangarembga's characters may be nervous, but this frothy mix of bourbon and pineapple juice will leave you anything but. Grab a glass of this fortifying blend and dive into her classic novel. We promise you won't regret it.

THE
TSITSI DANGAREMBGA COCKTAIL

Recipe
- 2 ½ fl oz pineapple juice
- 1 ½ fl oz bourbon
- 1 egg white
- lime peel to garnish

In a cocktail shaker, combine juice, bourbon, and egg white. Shake until combined. Add ice and shake again until frothy. Strain into a chilled lowball glass. Run a twist of lime peel along the rim and toss in for garnish.

Notable works:
Nervous Conditions, The Book of Not, Neria

CHIMAMANDA NGOZI ADICHIE

1977 – Present

Born in 1977, Chimamanda Ngozi Adichie is a world-renowned Nigerian author who we love for her memorable characters and feminist themes. Before gaining literary fame with her novels, Adichie won several short story awards, including an O. Henry Prize. Her first novel, the 2003 *Purple Hibiscus*, won a Commonwealth Writer's prize for best first book. It is a great example of the feminist content we have come to expect from Adichie: the book follows a teenage girl growing up in unstable postcolonial Nigeria under the religious and patriarchal oppression of her abusive father. Adichie's second novel, *Half of a Yellow Sun*, was likewise critically and commercially successful, winning the 2007 Orange Prize for Fiction, and gaining a spot on the *New York Time's* '100 Most Notable Books of the Year'. Set in 1960s Nigeria in the context of the Nigerian Civil War, it is full of characters whose identities are built in embracing and resisting their increasingly violent social and political circumstances.

We also love her talks 'The Danger of a Single Story' about the risk of creating singular cultural narratives, and 'We should all be feminists'. And let's not forget her latest novel, *Americanah*, which is a brilliant exploration of what it means to be black in Nigeria, the UK and America.

To honour this wonderful writer, we've created a complex drink that is both tart and sweet. If you can, garnish it with a purple edible flower as a reference to the purple hibiscus that represents freedom and individuality in Adichie's first novel.

THE
CHIMAMANDA NGOZI ADICHIE COCKTAIL

Recipe
- 1 ½ fl oz coconut rum
- 1 fl oz lychee juice
- ½ fl oz lime juice
- edible flower to garnish

In a cocktail shaker, combine rum, lychee juice, and lime juice. Shake with ice and strain into a chilled martini glass. Garnish, if you can, with a purple edible flower, such as a violet.

Notable works:
Purple Hibiscus, Half of a Yellow Sun, Americanah

ISABEL ALLENDE

1942 – Present

Isabel Allende is a Chilean-American writer born in Peru in 1942. She writes in Spanish, but her novels have been translated the world over. Allende writes primarily historical fiction that is well-known for often containing elements of magical realism. Allende received Chile's National Literature Prize in 2010.

Some of Allende's best-known works are *The House of Spirits* and *City of Beasts*, but our personal recommendation is *Island Beneath the Sea* (*La Isla Bajo el Mar*). The novel follows the life and struggles of Tete, a slave who eventually becomes a free woman. Allende's novels often contain many threads that braid together to tell one strong, compelling story. She puts a strong focus on female characters in her stories. We love the strength of her characters and the stories they tell for themselves.

Allende's cocktail is a version of a Chilean classic. Port wine, whisky, egg yolk, and spice combine in the Isabel Allende cocktail to present you with a heady, rich drink.

THE
ISABEL ALLENDE COCKTAIL

Recipe
- 1 fl oz port wine
- 1 fl oz whisky
- 1 egg yolk (very fresh)
- 1 tsp sugar
- dash Angora bitters
- cinnamon sugar (to top)
- cocoa powder (to top)

Whisk together until completely blended. Pour into a glass over a generous amount of ice. Sprinkle with cinnamon sugar and cocoa powder.

Notable works:
The House of Spirits, City of Beasts, Island Beneath the Sea, The Japanese Lover, Eva Luna, Daughter of Fortune

ENHEDUANNA
2285 – 2250 BC

If you haven't heard of this writer, we won't blame you. Considered by many scholars to be the world's first known author and poet, Enheduanna lived in the ancient Sumerian city-state of Ur during the 23rd century, BC. As a priestess, she produced a prolific body of literary work over the course of her lifetime, including devotions to the goddess Innana and the Sumerian Temple Hymns, which survive in the form of 37 stone tablets. These later copies of her work suggest that her hymns were valued and used for hundreds of years after her death. She was also the first woman known to hold the title of EN, or High Priestess, a position of both religious and political power in ancient Sumer. Despite being such a significant figure in literary history, Enheduanna is little acknowledged today.

We've decided to celebrate her here with a bloody orange twist on the classic Negroni. Rich red in colour and bitter as sin, this drink is truly fit for a High Priestess.

THE
ENHEDUANNA
COCKTAIL

Recipe
- 1 fl oz gin
- 1 fl oz Campari
- 1 fl oz sweet vermouth
- 1 fl oz fresh blood
  orange juice
- orange twist to garnish

Combine gin, Campari, vermouth, and juice. Pour over ice in a chilled lowball glass. Garnish with a twist of orange peel.

Notable works:
The Exaltation of Inanna, In-nin ša-gur-ra, The Sumerian Temple Hymns, Hymn to Nanna

The Karen Blixen cocktail, page 98

About the authors

Laura Becherer studied at the Universities of Wisconsin Platteville and Eau Claire and is currently working on her first novel as part of a DFA at the University of Glasgow.

Cameo Marlatt studied at Queen's University, Canada and the University of Edinburgh, and she is now studying towards a DFA at the University of Glasgow.

Acknowledgements

We would like to acknowledge the support of our friends, our families, and our classmates at the University of Glasgow. Thank you for faithfully attending our many cocktail parties, supplying us with generous quantities of alcohol, and allowing us to test even our most experimental recipes on you. We are grateful for your enthusiasm and encouragement throughout the project, and couldn't have done this without your discerning taste buds. Specifically, we would like to thank Samantha Becherer for her help and support, Ieuan Ledger for contributing to the Ursula Le Guin cocktail, Ruth Lockwood for contributing to the Alice Walker cocktail, and Carly Brown for suggestions on the Emily Dickinson cocktail. Additionally, we would like to thank our tutor Zoë Strachan for her suggestions on the Mary Shelley cocktail, and for providing us with advice and support from pitch to publication.

Huge thanks to James and Louise Rusk and the all the staff at Hutchesons Bar and Brasserie, Ingram Street, Glasgow, for their outstanding cocktail making skills and for providing such an elegant location for our cocktail photography.